DANIEL O'CONNELL
and his world

R. DUDLEY EDWARDS

DANIEL O'CONNELL

and his world

THAMES AND HUDSON

LONDON

Printed and bound in Great Britain by
Jarrold and Sons Ltd, Norwich

This is the story of the Irishman whose successful effort to secure political equality for his fellow countrymen through the Catholic Emancipation Act of 1829 led them to believe that he was the Moses who would deliver them from the bondage of British Protestantism. Daniel O'Connell was not the first to expound Irish nationality, but his influence upon his own generation was comparable to that of George Washington with the liberty-loving colonists in New England. O'Connell, unlike Washington, failed to achieve the ultimate victory which, to him, could only be achieved by a non-violent movement of moral force. When he failed, some of his followers took up the struggle in a more violent way which had little immediate effect beyond exacerbating the relations between Britain and Ireland, although it won for them the tolerant admiration which in Ireland has always been given to men of courage, prepared to vindicate their patriotic ideas by the sacrifice of their own lives. But O'Connell was also a divisive force as his achievement of Catholic emancipation, and his use of the clergy to organize the people, alienated most of the Protestants from his movement for the repeal of the legislative union with Great Britain, and for the re-establishment of an independent Irish parliament.

It is evident from O'Connell's speeches and writings that most modern ideas, right as well as wrong, on Irish nationalism, emanated in his time and from him. This book attempts to express the ideas of his world as briefly as possible, presented in a wealth of illustrative matter to give a greater reality to the reader. With the publication by Professor M. R. O'Connell of his ancestor's correspondence, the necessity for a much fuller treatment of the subject will become generally accepted.

The author has much pleasure in putting on record his indebtedness to his colleagues in University College, Dublin, especially in its Archives Department, and in the first instance to Miss D. McMahon. He would also like to record his conviction that the work could not have been completed without the continual co-operation of Miss A. C. Holland and Miss A. Ireland, as well as of his wife, Síle, and daughter, Ruth. Among the many others to whom the author is indebted, he would like to acknowledge those whose works are listed in the select bibliography and also the custodians of the historical collections in the National Museum of Ireland, and of the principal libraries and repositories in Dublin. A very special word of appreciation is due to the publishers.

R. DUDLEY EDWARDS   *20 December 1974*

"NO·MAN·HAS·A·RIGHT·TO·FIX·THE·
BOUNDARY·TO·THE·MARCH·OF·A·NATION·
NO·MAN·HAS·A·RIGHT·
TO·SAY·TO·HIS·COUNTRY·
THUS·FAR·SHALT·THOU·
GO·AND·NO·FURTHER·
WE·HAVE·NEVER·
ATTEMPTED·TO·FIX·
THE·NE·PLUS·ULTRA·
TO·THE·PROGRESS·OF·
IRELANDS·NATIONHOOD·
AND·WE·NEVER·SHALL".

The archetypal statement of Ireland's nationhood, in the words of Charles Stewart Parnell, is carved on the Parnell monument in Dublin.

IF NATIONALISM IS A PREDOMINANT FEATURE of history since the eighteenth-century revolutions, it is rather important to realize what a strong force in political unification nationalism has been in some countries long before the revolutionary epoch. When Henry Grattan, on the occasion of the Irish parliamentary declaration of independence, made reference to the existence of an Irish nation he was speaking in terms of a self-governing state, even though that state were associated with another through its monarchical head. Over large parts of western Europe, the reigning dynasties had been identified with the unification of their states and it is reasonable in the case of France to regard the monarchy as having achieved this. When Louis XVI was put on trial and described as Louis Capet, this was an implied acceptance of the belief that the people of France had been bound together under the monarchy which had existed among the Franks in the fifth century. Concurrently it could be said that the British monarchy had existed since the Anglo-Saxons invaded Britain in the fifth century. As the doctrine that the people were entitled to regulate their political affairs and choose their own rulers became more positively asserted in the eighteenth century, the idea of a nation as a political and cultural unit gained increasing vogue.

It is equally important, however, to remember that such ideas associating a national people with a great tradition did not necessarily operate in the same way in any two instances. Who were the people of Ireland if Ireland was claimed to be a nation? Was its great tradition distinct from that of the British people? Henry Grattan saluted the spirit of Swift and Molyneux as having been identified with assertions of the independence of Ireland. It might well have been embarrassing

Portrait of Christ from the Book of Kells: a ninth-century artist's conception of the divinely inspired leader.

for Grattan to refer to earlier personalities, as the sense of political unity in Ireland since the Reformation had been linked with a tradition unknown to Grattan and his fellow patriots. Irish nationalism could be said to have been a powerful sixteenth-century force which had become identified with Catholicism in the struggle against the English Protestant conquerors in the reign of Elizabeth Tudor.

In the development of a cultural tradition, political rivalries between conflicting elements in that tradition may make it difficult for those involved to recognize their cultural identity as easily as this may be recognized by outsiders or by an intellectual group among themselves. In ancient Ireland before the Anglo-Norman invasion, a group of warring peoples were given some sense of unity through the experience of being Christianized in the fifth and subsequent centuries. The Christian missionaries, brought up in the Roman tradition, gradually perceived the advantage of identifying the ancient Irish traditions with the people of the Book, the chosen people of God, whose Bible provided the written record of the divinely inspired traditions which kept Christians apart from everyone else. The ancient Irish tribal stories are of heroes and kings descended from a Celtic mythology which was transformed in the process of being set down in writing, made to conform to the Christian tradition, and unified in a legendary story of the occupation of Ireland by peoples identifiable in the Old Testament as having been connected with the chosen people of God. As the custodians of the written tradition were still centred in settlements of Latin learning at the time of the Viking invasions, it was relatively easy to assert the unity of Christian Ireland against these pagan invaders. It was equally possible at the time of the Anglo-Norman invasion to recognize that the Irish people accepted the primacy of the Pope, who might advise them on their religious and cultural organization. From the time of Henry II, the papal donations of the title of Lord of Ireland to the Plantagenet rulers created a sense of Irishness distinct from the rest of the Anglo-Norman domains. By the time that Henry VIII severed the connection between England and the papacy, the significance in Ireland of the Holy See had been sufficient to maintain this separate tradition, though undeniably the papacy had often used its influence on the side of the kings of England against rebellious Irish kings and lords. It was thus possible in Ireland, when Rome attempted to discipline the Tudor schismatic and heretical rulers, to establish a papal party, and in the English wars of conquest to preserve the legends and stories of the fighters for Irish Catholic freedom. Thus by the seventeenth century, when Protestantism and nationalism had become associated in England, Catholicism and nationalism had become associated in Ireland.

The first attempted political unification of the Three Kingdoms of England, Ireland and Scotland when James VI of Scotland succeeded to the English and Irish kingdoms of Elizabeth I, did not come about without a civil war which became part of the great religious struggle of the Thirty Years War in Europe. If that war came to an end with the successful defeat of the Stuart monarchy and the setting up of the Protestant Commonwealth of England, under the victorious Oliver Cromwell who subdued also the Irish and the Scots, it left a permanent mark on the history of Ireland by linking the Stuarts to an Irish national tradition and imposing a new Protestant colonial class who gained control of the greater part of the landed property of Ireland. They became linked with Britain as the colonial upper crust of society. Hardly had James II been defeated in Ireland and the colonial Ascendancy confirmed when resentment towards the English government for regarding the colonists in Ireland as subordinate led to the assertion by William Molyneux that parliamentary

Henry Grattan, leader of the Irish
House of Commons and fighter for
Ireland's national integrity.

liberties had existed in Ireland since the time of Henry II; it was this
assertion which caused Grattan to acclaim Molyneux as an Irish
national evangelist.

When, a generation later, Jonathan Swift attacked English government in Ireland for treating the people as unworthy of the rights of
freemen, Swift so reasserted the individuality of the people in Ireland
that he in turn earned from Grattan recognition as a national evangelist. The people of Molyneux and of Swift, however, were only the
colonial element, from whom were excluded the Catholic majority
who had been involved against William of Orange and the revolutionary forces of 1689. By the time of Grattan, the concept of the
people of Ireland was only just beginning to change. The Catholics,
having been prepared to follow the Pope in abandoning the Stuarts,
were being gradually admitted to the privileges of citizenship but they
were still regarded with such qualification that their admission to full
political powers was not thought proper. Slowly the idea that the
Catholics deserved political emancipation gathered support, though
from the very beginning this encountered hostility from those opposed
to power-sharing and by those who feared that the Catholics would
use emancipation to take the estates from the Protestants. By the end
of the American War of Independence, the question of parliamentary

reform provoked different reactions in Ireland from those in England, though even in Britain the first measures of Catholic relief provoked the Gordon riots in 1780 in Edinburgh and in London. To many of the Irish Catholics, then, the forces of nationalism as represented by Grattan and his associates had little real significance. Grattan himself tended to become more liberal to Catholics but when the legislative union came about at the end of the century, Grattan's dirge over the death of the Irish nation was one in which few Catholics participated. Among those few, however, was that remarkable young lawyer Daniel O'Connell.

Daniel O'Connell is the most significant character in the history of Irish nationalism, considered in the context of the world revolution and counter-revolution in the last half of the eighteenth century and the first half of the nineteenth. It is important that we have some appreciation of these contemporary political events at the time of O'Connell's birth, as without this we cannot hope to put his career into any kind of historical perspective. O'Connell, as will be seen, was so completely the reflection of his era.

At the beginning of this period, western Europe's domination had extended to the other continents, and particularly to America. At the

Catholic emancipation was still an explosive question at the end of the eighteenth century. Under the slogan 'No Popery' the mob sacked and burned Newgate Prison in the Gordon Riots of 1780.

An age of revolution

In CONGRESS, July 4, 1776.

The unanimous Declaration of the thirteen united States of America.

America's Declaration of Independence, perhaps the most important formative influence of O'Connell's early life. What the founding fathers wrote about governments 'deriving their just powers from the consent of the governed' could have come from the Liberator himself.

end of the period, the rivalries between the western European states had precipitated revolution and the setting up overseas of many former subject colonies as independent states. The English hegemony established in America after the conclusion of the Seven Years War was to crumble away within two decades. The American War of Independence which broke out in the year after O'Connell's birth had a galvanizing effect on the *anciens régimes* of Europe, and the consciousness of revolutionary America increasingly influenced not only European international politics but also domestic developments in various countries. The French general Lafayette became an international personality after his return from assisting the Americans. However, a sense of the greatness of America was not to become evident in international rivalries until the end of O'Connell's lifetime.

O'Connell's career must be placed against this, the most influential event of his early life, and perhaps unconsciously, the most formative for him politically. He absorbed the libertarian and egalitarian principles of the American revolutionaries and he continued to advocate these throughout his career. O'Connell was thus very much a product of his age. But for the American Revolution, O'Connell would probably have become, like so many of his co-religionists, including his uncle, a self-exiled Irishman, professionally employed by some foreign Catholic power. But the more egalitarian atmosphere which came about after the American Revolution gave to him, as to others in Great Britain and Ireland, a career open to talents which would probably have been denied in other circumstances. 'It is an age of revolution,' said Tom Paine, 'in which everything may be looked for.'

The government of Ireland in the eighteenth century was conducted by the viceregal representative of the Hanoverian King of Great Britain, who utilized his kingdom of Ireland to strengthen his limited resources as a constitutional monarch. Since the revolution of 1689, which necessitated power-sharing with the British landed aristocracy and commercial magnates, monarchy was restricted in its military power and obliged in Britain to maintain its position through parliament's financial control. This necessitated regular resort by the King's ministers to parliamentary sanction of taxation. The Hanoverian monarchs had, of course, more influence in foreign affairs and to a large extent this also applied to Ireland and the colonies. Since the accession of George III, the monarchy was represented as more British and less Germanic and the King's friends revived the old Tory traditions of the alliance of the people and of the episcopalian Protestant Church with the monarchy. The Viceroy in Ireland customarily conducted business by making an informal arrangement with leading parliamentarians, the so-called Undertakers, who undertook to secure acquiescent majorities in the House of Lords and the House of Commons in return for a substantial part of government patronage. Occasionally difficulties arose, mainly because of clashes between parliamentary personalities. In their differences, these were inclined to exploit sensitivities noticeable in some public questions where the subordination of the Irish state appeared to be particularly unjustifiable, by contrast with relative situations in England where the powers of parliament had so markedly increased since 1689. Thus in the 1720s the Viceroy was embarrassed by a public outcry against the grant to an Englishman named Wood of a monopoly for issuing copper coinage for Ireland. In the 1750s, similarly, the anxiety of parliament to be consulted over a financial surplus again provoked a popular outburst. Under George III, difficulties with the Undertakers led to a decision to restrict patronage to the Viceroy. In consequence these Undertakers took up constitutional questions such as the restriction of the duration of parliament. This created, on the eve of the American War of Independence, resentment in Ireland against

George III: marble bust by Edward
Smyth.

the methods of government and favoured to some extent the American
viewpoint expressing objection to 'taxation without representation'
when the English parliament imposed taxes on the American
colonists. In Ireland, however, the viceregal power was sufficiently
strong for most purposes to secure for the government resolutions of
loyalty when the American colonists resorted to violence and went
into rebellion against Great Britain.

The situation in America of course deteriorated when the government proceeded to extremes in asserting that opposition was treasonable against the King. In the long run such tactics strengthened the
American forces of opposition and led to the setting up of an independent republic where monarchy and, in particular, King George
III, appeared to be tyrannical. This legend, however, of monarchical
tyranny was not found in Ireland among the critics of the government.
Expressions of loyalty to His Majesty continued to be offered while
opportunities were sought to secure more parliamentary powers in
Ireland, particularly after the exponents in England of peace with
America expressed their readiness to support wider constitutional
liberties for the colonies. Again, after France intervened on the side
of America, leading Irish parliamentarians such as Henry Grattan
claimed that as England's only loyal ally Ireland should be conceded
the same constitutional liberties proposed for America. Simul-

taneously, groups and committees of Catholics in Ireland, excluded from many constitutional privileges because of their alleged devotion to the exiled Stuarts as well as to the Pope, expressed themselves in most humble terms of loyalty to their Hanoverian ruler, to whom they subscribed an oath of allegiance in large numbers after some relaxation of the anti-Catholic Penal Laws in 1778.

In these circumstances, in the year before the international recognition of American independence, the Irish parliament was admitted by the government to legislative independence. Thereafter it might be said that Ireland was ruled by its King, Lords and Commons. The influence of America had undoubtedly contributed to this changed state of affairs but it does not appear to have influenced any outstanding personalities to taking up a republican position.

It is important in reading contemporary statements, however, not to accept them uncritically. To the monarchical European world, republicanism smacked of treason. Successive American diplomatic representatives at European courts before the outbreak of the French Revolution were regarded with the same curiosity as that accorded to Soviet diplomats after World War I. Among the intelligentsia, republicanism was generally favoured but obeisance to monarchical protocol was only to be expected from people in public life. However, republicanism was much evident among young students in the

The Viceregal Lodge in Phoenix Park, near Dublin. From here, before the setting up of an independent parliament in 1922, Ireland was governed. It is now the official home of the President.

universities and in the law courts, before they were absorbed into one establishment or another. It did not so spur O'Connell and there is little evidence that he was in any way infected by the prevailing republicanism which swayed so many of his fellow law students.

Having set out the political background to our subject, we must now look to an equally formative sphere, his family.

The O'Connells of Kerry

On 6 August 1775, Daniel O'Connell was born at Carhen, Cahirciveen, Co. Kerry, the son of a modest landed proprietor, Morgan O'Connell, one of whose brothers Maurice, colloquially known as 'Hunting Cap', was a larger landowner at Derrynane Abbey on the other side of Cahirciveen. A third brother, Daniel O'Connell, had risen in the French royal army to be a colonel of an Irish regiment, later became a general and was created a Count of France.

The O'Connells were relatively insignificant before the late eighteenth century but they could trace their ancestry to seventeenth-century personalities in the country of MacCarthy More, for whom they held the wardenship of an important castle. In retrospect, however, the most outstanding O'Connell of the seventeenth century was the Capuchin Franciscan Daniel Robert O'Connell, joint author with Barnaby Richard O'Ferrall of *Commentarius Rinuccinianus*, the historical account of the papal nunciature of John Baptist Rinuccini

Derrynane Abbey, which O'Connell was eventually to inherit from his uncle, Maurice 'Hunting Cap' O'Connell.

to the Irish Catholic Confederates at Kilkenny in their war against the English in the 1640s.

Of the O'Connells, it was remarked in the nineteenth century by the historian John O'Donovan that they were not represented in the Irish genealogical tradition. The implication of this is that they were without political significance. After the emergence of Daniel O'Connell, the subject of this biography, their significance among the landed gentry became sufficient for them to appear in the lists of the officers-of-arms who authenticated pedigrees (perhaps without over-much attention to scholarship). That Count O'Connell was a person of some eminence who could lend lustre from exile on his Irish relatives is undoubted. That his brother 'Hunting Cap' established himself somewhat like an ancient chieftain at Derrynane seems to have followed from his remarkable capacity in the accumulation of wealth, partly due to unusual business aptitude and partly due to successful smuggling. 'Hunting Cap', at the instance of his brother the Count, adopted and educated his nephew Daniel, sending him to France to St Omer and Douai, where he received the education of an English Catholic exile until the French revolutionary wars closed these institutions. Daniel O'Connell then transferred to London where he attended law courses in preparation for a career at the Bar.

Life in Ireland in Co. Kerry in the days of 'Hunting Cap' was little affected by the anglicization which had transformed the upper class. The O'Connells were anxious to be on good terms with their well-to-do and better-known neighbours, such as the Knight of Kerry, Lord Kenmare and Lord Lansdowne. These of course were in the politically conscious element of the nation, and through them 'Hunting Cap' was hopeful of being appointed to titular posts of honour, such as Deputy Lieutenant of the county. The position, however, was a little delicate as the Irish Catholics, since the defeat of James II, were regarded as of doubtful loyalty. The Penal Laws against Catholics, passed at the instance of the Irish parliament, restricted position, authority and office to those prepared to deny Roman Catholic doctrines and abjure the exiled Stuart king. However, on the death of the son of James II – who claimed to be James III – in 1766 the papacy avoided recognizing his heir. Irish Catholics, led by their bishops, publicly prayed for the Hanoverian royal family and many of them subscribed to the oath of allegiance, which enabled Catholics increasingly to take their part in society. Political power was not so easily conceded and the right to vote in parliamentary elections was as far as the government and the Irish parliament were prepared to go, with the result that Catholics were still excluded from membership of parliament at the Union of legislatures in 1800.

In Co. Kerry, a Catholic family such as the O'Connells then had little connection with major politics. To a large extent, the leading members of the family, while possessing a knowledge of the English

Daniel, Count O'Connell, uncle of
the Liberator. He rose to general's
rank in the French army.

language, participated in the Gaelic traditions which still survived.
The O'Connells themselves included several Irish poets with a little
talent, and Daniel recorded in his diary in the 1790s, apropos of
Macpherson's Ossian, that many of these stories and songs had been
known to him in his childhood in Kerry.

The O'Connells in France, like other Irish and English exiles, were
concerned to serve loyally the royal governments which gave them
hospitality and advanced them. Inevitably they stressed their gentle
antecedents, if only because promotion to higher ranks in the army, as
in the Church, was confined under the *ancien régime* to those whose
claims to bear arms were recognized in their countries of origin or by
surviving officers-of-arms of the exiled Stuarts. From the middle of
the eighteenth century, the Hanoverian officers-of-arms regularly
facilitated exiles seeking substantiation for their claims. In France,
Count O'Connell was an upholder of monarchy and inevitably with
the outbreak of the French Revolution he joined the French royal
émigrés in England. The O'Connells thus identified with the English
monarchical tradition whose government gave refuge and hospitality
to those who withdrew from France after the fall of the old regime and
the establishment of the Republic.

It is thus that the attitude in Kerry of the O'Connells became more
closely identified with the English conservative tradition. When
Daniel O'Connell, the law student in England, concerned himself
with cultural matters, they were inevitably the interests and concerns
of an educated English gentleman. As a lawyer, of course, he was led
to interest himself in the political writings of the time, in which the
advocacy of egalitarianism was particularly strong. It is clear from
O'Connell's diary that he associated freely with young English
lawyers and his occasional personal comment regarding religious
convictions leave one in little doubt that he was infected by the prevailing deism. Until he returned to Ireland, however, he does not
appear to have been faced with any serious personal crisis of conscience.
His return coincided with the major impact of the French Revolution.

O'Connell shared with many of the Irish of the south-west a
remarkable capacity in conversation to identify himself with the views
of those he was anxious to placate. This identification might be no
more than would be regarded as proper politeness. It could also
represent O'Connell's own views to a considerable extent, though
he might well find himself, in different situations in a relatively short
space of time, acquiescing in different viewpoints. The young student
who had fled from France as the revolutionaries in 1793 drove them
out of their colleges, was more of a monarchist than perhaps he was
subsequently as a law student in England. In his later days, he was a
strong advocate of constitutional monarchy.

O'Connell has left on record his opinions on a variety of questions,
in letters, in speeches, in writings, both for private purposes and for

publication. Despite the wealth of these, it is always necessary to treat each individual document and statement critically, with special awareness of O'Connell's remarkable capacity to relate to his audience, individually or collectively. It may even be hazarded that he did not entirely know his own mind and that in the ultimate analysis, if his powerful personality could not dominate a situation, it was because he was unsure or without the impulse to grapple with the event.

In a certain sense, O'Connell the lawyer departed radically from the conservative attitudes of his Kerry relations and of his *émigré* uncle, who respected monarchy and distrusted parliamentarianism. One of Daniel O'Connell's great achievements was that he linked the Catholic emancipation movement to parliamentary traditions.

It is clear from O'Connell's correspondence as a law student with his uncle in Kerry that he had clear ideas of his unusual abilities and of the way to go about exploiting them. His uncle, 'Hunting Cap', was very slow to spend money which could be put away, and the nephew placated him in order to secure the resources for his education. He assured his uncle that he had come to realize that he was possessed of a boundless ambition and that he could succeed in his career by profound study, which would enable him to acquire much knowledge of society, so that he might carry out the functions of a gentleman. His acceptance as a lawyer would help him to undertake these.

O'Connell's realization of his capacity to utilize the knowledge he had acquired in his studies enabled him to judge very coolly how far his own achievements excelled his fellow law students in debate. He was able, at this early stage, to gauge his own character and thus he succeeded in restricting his participation in social festivities in order to devote himself more systematically to study, once he became aware that he had the gift of being able to attract others by his wit, his charm, his quickness in repartee and through his habit of retailing stories of his own experiences and the gossip about contemporary men of interest. O'Connell's self-possession has been remarked upon in many situations and this enabled him to use the advantages of his fine physical appearance to dominate on most occasions.

In the diary he kept in his early days as a law student and a lawyer, he displays some reticence in analysing his own character. That he was ambitious to an unusual degree, and that he was expected to be so, emerges clearly. It is also evident that he was conscious of his social gifts, which enabled him to play an adequate part with others in any society in which he was accepted. He seemed well aware of his attractiveness to women and he was greatly drawn to feminine society, easily susceptible, but perhaps a little unsure of himself.

From successes in court, where his remarkable abilities enabled him to outwit the less gifted on the judicial bench and among the lawyers to secure the acquittal of clients so frequently that he earned

Daniel O'Connell as a young man: self-possession and a fine physical appearance.

the reputation of being able to win even in the most hopeless cases, he proceeded to win an even greater reputation at public meetings.

Almost inevitably these meetings were concerned with the Catholic question, where O'Connell associated with old campaigners like John Keogh, and Protestants who had interested themselves in the movement, which some of them, like Henry Parnell and Grattan, continued to support when the opportunity offered. To many of these O'Connell was not a man of importance, however versatile and active on the various occasions when efforts were being made to secure some fresh approach to the question. O'Connell's remarkably resonant voice, his easy success in winning a meeting to his viewpoint, so frequently brought about by his air of confidence, led him to be regarded more significantly than would more ordinary men in their early thirties.

O'Connell's interventions on the Catholic question carried authority through his capacity to express with self-assurance the issues as being no more than a concession of public justice for a substantial popular element in the community. His leadership became increasingly acceptable as older Catholic personalities, only too mindful of former adversities in the days of the 1798 rebellion, lacked his initiative and courage. O'Connell's self-assurance as a lawyer was also valuable in gaining the support of the higher clergy who, with the nobility, had habitually relied upon government patronage and distrusted the parliamentarians and the radicals. His capacity to give confidence to the clergy led to a situation in which Catholic interests in Ireland asserted themselves effectively when the English Catholics, following the Whig Protestants in the emancipation movement, accepted the veto proposal. O'Connell was thus in a position to direct public attention to the Irish dimension in the Catholic question and to insist that on matters of politics, Rome could not prevail before what was necessary at home.

In this matter, O'Connell revealed his perceptiveness. The clergy for generations had been the comforters of the people in their political distress. To convert them into the agents of Dublin Castle would have led, quickly, to their rejection by the people. O'Connell could be a moderating influence when necessary, particularly on uncertain grounds. In seeing through the Catholic question to its Irish dimension he realized how different things were in Ireland, where the forces of law and order were distrusted by the people. Gradually O'Connell came to see that his influence with most of the Irish clergy was so positive that he could provide them with a wider role in society, in which at his direction they would act as the organizers of the Catholic movement at the local level.

O'Connell's capacity for work was remarkable and over the greater part of his career he devoted many hours every morning to the accumulation of the necessary information on any case in which he was con-

Souvenir glass goblet, offering 'a hundred thousand welcomes' to the King in Gaelic.

cerned and in the mastery of it. Coming to the conclusion that the clergy could be relied upon to provide the local leadership for a popular movement, he adopted the principle that the people could actively participate in politics by making subscriptions to the Catholic Association for the nominal sum of a shilling a year. It was a decision taken after the Protestant challenge had been thrown down with the cry of 'No popery' when the Hanoverian dynasty accepted the role of leaders of the Protestant nation.

In O'Connell's character, to some contemporaries, there was an element of obsequiousness and servility which contrasted distastefully with the arrogance and the defiance he habitually employed in the law courts and at meetings. Byron derided him for his behaviour when George IV visited Ireland soon after his coronation. O'Connell was perhaps sensitive on the charge of servility and denied subsequently some of the statements attributed to him when he presented a laurel wreath to the King on his departure from Dun Laoghaire, thereafter named Kingstown in his honour. In the short term, the King's expression of satisfaction at his reception by his Irish people, Protestant and Catholic, was particularly gratifying to O'Connell who had seen the occasion as one which forwarded his policy of combining all creeds in giving the King an Irish welcome. Sir Walter Scott showed comparable insight in welcoming the monarch on his visit to Edinburgh. Each of them discerned the value of associating the dynasty with his people. In Ireland the King's letter to his people was translated into Gaelic by Connellan, his Irish historiographer. Perhaps

The triumphal entry of George IV into Dublin, soon after his coronation. Byron ridiculed O'Connell for obsequiousness to the defender of the Protestant faith. 'Wear, Fingal, thy trapping! O'Connell, proclaim/His accomplishments! *His!!!*'

O'Connell's obsequiousness revealed his greater understanding of royal assumptions than a Byron could have understood. In the long run, O'Connell had the mortification of realizing his miscalculation, as the King and his royal brothers of York and Clarence identified themselves with 'No popery', perhaps because they sought a popularity among ordinary Protestants denied them in their earlier discreditable days. The evangelical revival accentuated the Protestant bitterness towards Catholicism. It probably, too, in reaction, played a part in strengthening O'Connell's decision to use the Catholic clergy as instruments in organizing the people in the national campaign which, but for O'Connell, would not have been won in 1829. We cannot be quite sure that the Liberator saw clearly how to bring about this achievement. There can be no doubt, however, that he knew how to inspire the nation-wide revolt of the forty-shilling freeholders, the mass of ordinary Catholic electors with the right to exercise the parliamentary franchise. This enabled O'Connell to answer the royal support for 'No popery' by making the Catholics of Ireland the decisive people in the winning of emancipation.

O'Connell's very success with the people reacted adversely in England with the Whigs and with the Catholics. The latter disliked the vulgarity of his popular performances. The former, who at first had been attracted by his moderation and his manner, became more reserved as the Irishman's exuberance seemed likely to be employed in English situations as well as on his home ground. It was here that O'Connell's chameleon-like characteristics of adapting himself differently to different situations enabled him to recover somewhat with the politicians, though aristocratic English Catholicism was to remain alienated. Even at home the embarrassment of being expected to follow his direction probably contributed to the Irish hierarchy's attribution to Wellington rather than to O'Connell of the credit for Catholic relief in 1829.

Arthur, Duke of Wellington: portrait by John Lucas. The Church gave more credit to him than to O'Connell for Catholic relief in 1829.

O'Connell's marriage to Mary O'Connell, his 'penniless' cousin, as their descendant, Professor M.R. O'Connell, has described her, is probably an important clue to the understanding of his character. By failing to make a marriage which would enrich him financially, O'Connell jeopardized his chances to secure the inheritance of his wealthy uncle Maurice of Derrynane. Mary's gifts were, however, far more necessary to him. She had no brilliance, could in no way outshine him, but was an admirable recipient for all his confidences. She provided, in addition to their substantial family, a wealth of common-sense and down-to-earth devotion to his family, to his interests, to his career. There is plenty of evidence that O'Connell greatly enjoyed reliving the triumphs he won in narrating them to her, and in the enjoyment of her reciprocity, often expressed in pedestrian terms contrasting markedly with his own lively prose.

Part of a letter from Mary to Daniel illustrates both her devotion and her practicality – '. . . those three days, my Love that you will spend in Tralee, before the assizes commences, you would spend here, were it not for its being such a lenght of way, and so bad a road but as you are well I am satisfied . . .'

Mary O'Connell, 'an admirable recipient for all his confidences'.

Daniel O'Connell was a great family man and his exuberant affection brims over continually in his correspondence. He had an understandably great pride in the modest achievements of his sons. He was particularly attached to his daughters, but with all his children he exacted standards of conduct befitting the children of an Irish states-man. They appear to have accepted their various roles in society and understood that it was for their father to determine their positions in public life. Beyond his immediate descendants – for there were many grandchildren – he maintained a keen interest in all his relatives from Kerry and Cork, and his wife occasionally rallied him for his softness in parting easily with money to them, implying that in his constant visits to Kerry, he invariably returned penniless.

O'Connell has been the subject of sophisticated gossip for alleged sexual activities beyond the bounds of marriage. Possibly the most

Lord Melbourne, the Whig Prime Minister. Like O'Connell, he too was the subject of salacious gossip.

extreme and unprovable allegation was that if a stone was thrown over the wall of any southern Irish workhouse, it would probably hit one of his bastards. In Kerry folklore, there is no reflection of such gossip. As Professor Helen Mulvey points out, in her essay on O'Connell's family in the new edition of correspondence edited by Professor M. R. O'Connell, such allegations run contrary to the trend of the letters. Undoubtedly, the great man's susceptibility to women was occasion-ally a cause of anxiety to his wife, notably regarding a governess of his daughters. O'Connell had evidently told Mary something of at least one pre-matrimonial affair. On an occasion when she appeared to have thought that he might feel himself obliged to contribute finan-cially to one of these old flames, she expressed herself tactfully about the need to consider his own financial difficulties and the consequen-tial restrictions on what was due to their children.

In the early 1830s, English Tory society derived some satisfaction when the Whig Prime Minister, Melbourne, was involved in an action for criminal correspondence with Mrs Norton. Perhaps Melbourne was lucky to escape with no legal stain on his character.

William Pitt the Younger, under whose ministry the Act of Union was passed.

O'Connell, too, was perhaps lucky to escape when the London *Times* took up the case of Ellen Courtenay. She claimed O'Connell had seduced her in Dublin more than twenty years earlier and that he was the father of the son that she had to support. The *Times* publicity given to encounters on the street between O'Connell and Miss Courtenay's son, allegedly beaten off by the Liberator's lawful progeny, did not result in fixing any permanent scandal on him, though it may well have contributed to the growth of the legend of his sexual prowess, particularly among Irish Protestants.

The United Irishmen and Emmet

The loss of the American colonies seriously discredited the government of King George III. The Whigs, who had opposed the government of the King's friends, had to be brought into office and some part of their programme for parliamentary reform was adopted. A degree of instability, however, persisted until the succession as Prime Minister of the remarkably able William Pitt, son of the renowned Earl of Chatham.

Charles James Fox. As a Whig, in opposition to Pitt, he had great influence in Ireland.

In Ireland, the King's government was not sufficiently strong to prevent the passage of parliamentary resolutions to safeguard the monopoly of legislative power; accordingly, by an Act of 1784, the British parliament renounced all claims to legislate for Ireland and recognized the appellate jurisdiction of the Irish House of Lords in all suits of law. The government, however, was able to use its influence effectively against any substantial measure of reform in Ireland. It was not sufficiently strong to negotiate an economic treaty between the two kingdoms as the commercial interest of each was in conflict with the other; the Irish parliament was too sensitive to approve any revised propositions which seemed to be dictated by the English parliament.

Towards the end of the 1780s, the Irish parliament displayed its political ineptitude in the Regency crisis when the Prince of Wales, later George IV, had to take over when his father became insane. As the English government was rather nervous lest the Regent might seek to appoint to office his friends among the opposition, plans were afoot to restrict his powers in a way which did not accord with Irish parliamentary sensitivities. Thus a situation could have arisen in which the powers of the Regent would have been less circumscribed in Ireland than in England. Fortunately for Pitt, the King recovered and the embarrassment with the Regent terminated. But Pitt had learned for the second time that government in Ireland could become a serious difficulty if security was to be maintained in political crises. Although the main offices in Ireland continued to be filled in accordance with the prevailing views of the English Cabinet, the strength of the opposition Whigs was particularly strong in Ireland and Charles James Fox, probably with Edmund Burke and Pitt the most outstanding statesmen of their time, had considerable influence in Ireland. The influence of Fox was exercised with the Ponsonbys and with Grattan. The influence of Burke over the Catholics was also very considerable and was to play its part substantially in influencing them when Burke with Portland joined a coalition government under Pitt to fight the French Revolution.

As in England, the fall of the Bastille on 14 July 1789 was greeted with rejoicing in Ireland. As in England, as long as the constitutional changes which converted the Estates-General into a constituent assembly appeared to be proceeding along the lines of the English Revolution of 1688, this enthusiasm was maintained. When France, however, became dominated by republican sentiments, the number of admirers, in Ireland as in England, seriously diminished. The execution of Louis XVI and of his Queen, Marie Antoinette, was regarded with favour by few politically minded people in Ireland. The great indictment by Burke in his *Reflections on the French Revolution* probably carried the majority in Ireland as in England, and Pitt's declaration of war against the French republic would have had a substantial degree of popular support.

The taking of the Bastille, 14 July 1789, an event greeted with joy in Ireland, and in England, until the execution of Louis XVI and his Queen.

There was, however, in Ireland a considerable number of critics of the failure to secure a full measure of parliamentary reform. Irish Volunteers had been embodied and armed, somewhat reluctantly, by the government in the crisis of the American War of Independence and had utilized their unique opportunity to secure the popular demand for free trade and for legislative independence. When the Volunteers, led by Henry Flood, went on to claim that parliament should be reformed, they found themselves represented as a dictatorial military group attempting to overawe a legitimate legislature. Further efforts under Napper Tandy to establish an Irish Congress – using the American revolutionary term – also secured scant parliamentary support. Thus the spirit of reform languished, only to revive temporarily after the outbreak of the French Revolution. But the reform advocates were too weak to secure more than a very moderate measure to exclude government placemen from parliament. When the French Revolution abolished the monarchy, the various Irish political clubs,

Bantry Bay. Into this bay in the south-west Wolfe Tone sailed with a French fleet in 1796, but the attempt was defeated by storms.

Theobald Wolfe Tone, one of the founders of the United Irishmen, plotted to set up an independent Irish republic with the aid of a French invasion.

such as the United Irishmen, came close to despair at the failure to make parliament more democratic and responsible. With the outbreak of war between Great Britain and Ireland and the French Republic, the United Irishmen became a secret revolutionary body, convinced that the English government, and indeed the influence of England generally, was hostile to the best interests of Ireland. Theobald Wolfe Tone, the best-known United Irishman to subsequent generations, devoted himself to bringing about a French invasion to secure the establishment of a republic.

The history of the United Irishmen has been written in terms of the idealism of men who sought to substitute for sectarian animosities a common feeling of being Irish. In the context of the war with France this was unreal. The extent to which the French republican forces treated the institutions of organized religion as hostile inevitably led the overwhelming majority of those who put first the security of property to oppose them. The Bantry Bay expedition which threatened to invade Ireland led Maurice O'Connell to report the threat immediately to government officials in 1796. Viewing the whole matter from Dublin, Daniel O'Connell observed in his diary that the Irish were unfit for self-government and that a successful French invasion would be disastrous to the best interests of the country. It is important to remember that at this juncture O'Connell had all a young man's feelings for liberty and freedom. He claimed subsequently to have had some connection with the United Irishmen but it may be assumed that he avoided anything treasonable, and he was for a time careful not to be involved in situations where he might become the victim of suspicions and of allegations of disloyalty. Concurrently, he had become connected with various politically minded organizations in Dublin, including at least one debating society which enabled him to perfect his oratorical style in controversy. He was a member of a Freemason lodge in which he held office, probably because of his connections with the Irish Bar, to which he was called in 1798. He was also a member of a volunteer military organization, the yeomanry corps of the Dublin lawyers, in which capacity, as late as 1803 at the time of the Emmet insurrection, he was involved in sentry duty.

The rebellion of Robert Emmet in 1803 was condemned by O'Connell as a senseless outbreak and the murder of Arthur Wolfe, Lord Kilwarden, by Emmet's followers loomed largely in O'Connell's mind when he expressed himself in correspondence as convinced that Emmet's ill-conceived enterprise justified any punishment the State might impose upon it. What O'Connell was not to realize was that Emmet's speech from the dock would pass into history as one of the proudest examples of defiance of English misgovernment in Ireland.

Robert Emmet. 'When my country takes her place among the nations of the earth, then, and not till then, let my epitaph be written.'

Lord Kilwarden murdered by a mob of Emmet's followers in 1803. O'Connell at this time considered his countrymen unfit for self-government.

I acted as an Irishman, determined on delivering my country from this doubly-riveted despotism. I wished to place her independence beyond the reach of any power on earth. I wished to exalt her to that proud station in the world. . . . I wished to procure for my country the guarantee which Washington procured for America. . . . It was for these ends I sought aid from France.

Emmet's words would provide a model in the twentieth century for those who again took up arms against the government of the United Kingdom. Yet O'Connell had not abandoned his concepts of freedom nor his belief, like that of Emmet, in the right of Ireland to remain an independent state. For at the Union and contrary to the ideas of his uncle, 'Hunting Cap', O'Connell denounced the amalgamation of the legislatures and said that as a Catholic he would prefer to have the Penal Laws re-imposed rather than be a party to the extinction of the independent Irish parliament.

O'Connell's appeal to the Irish parliamentary opposition to the Union was not entirely the heroic gesture to the Protestant Ascendancy, the dominant upper-class colonial planters, which it might appear. He was aware that such a statement from a man of little political significance, and virtually outside public life in 1800, was unlikely to be treated as an invitation to re-enact the Penal Laws (passed to enslave the Catholics after the Williamite revolution of 1688 and modified and eased only in 1774). The rebellion of 1798 in some parts of the country, such as Wexford, had revealed evidence of the desire on the part of well-to-do farmers and rural workers to get rid of the landed aristocracy. This concomitant of revolution was to O'Connell an anathema. It helps to explain his preference for the propertied classes and his willingness to put his trust in the Protestant Ascendancy.

In one further particular, O'Connell's mind would seem to be moving into an anti-revolutionary position, perhaps in consequence of his support of the Catholic Committee. The French revolutionary attempt to express rationally the principles of political government had emerged as hostile to organized religion, as well as to monarchy. O'Connell would not see any reason in eradicating Catholic traditions in Ireland, which he would regard as enhancing Irish cultural prestige from the time of St Patrick. The republicanism of the United Irishmen may not have depended absolutely on the new French principles to the exclusion of ancient Irish cultural traditions, though the United Irishmen knew little about them. When the courageous young Emmet attacked his judges, he called in question the reality of British liberties in Ireland, obsessed as he was with public corruption. O'Connell was well aware of the reality of public corruption but did not believe it necessary to destroy the existing order. Aware that the English government which had subsidized Maynooth was prepared to go further in supporting the Church of his ancestors,

Connemara peasant's hut – engraving from the *Illustrated London News,* 1843. This was the other side of the coin of which the obverse was the well-to-do Protestant landlord.

O'Connell was bound to reject Emmet, whose principles and whose allies, if victorious, could bring down the Catholic Church in Ireland with the establishment. Nor was O'Connell alone in this view. Emmet's youth and his courage, his defiance of his judges and his austere direction that his epitaph should not be written while his country remained unfree preserved his memory. Few would have endorsed his political principles who were genuinely attached to the English constitutional tradition and to Christianity. If the claim that O'Connell was so attached is here put forward, it is not without documentary evidence. It cannot be asserted that the deism he affected as a law student was abandoned by any specific date. His public identification with the Catholic Church is evident from 1800. A more positive, almost public, participation in Church festivals emerges some ten years later. The rational decisions clearly were taken when O'Connell condemned the Revolution and condemned Emmet.

It is on record that O'Connell's uncle, 'Hunting Cap', had no such attachment to the Irish parliament. That realistic Kerryman saw clearly that Catholic emancipation before 1800 had depended on the Crown and on the King's advisers. Ironically, the Act of Union weakened the royal position in Ireland and made it more dependent upon parliament at Westminster. However little the later O'Connell felt favourable to Westminster, his action in opposing the Union, if

historically unjustifiable, denoted a political insight as regards the future denied to the older generation of O'Connells at home and abroad. And in the long run, it was the younger O'Connell who was to shape the minds and the actions of his people.

The career of Napoleon Bonaparte transformed the situation created in the war waged against the French Revolution by the states which upheld the *ancien régime*. The effective organization of victory by Carnot, the striking and decisive defeats of the greatest armies in Europe by Napoleon, put a premium on military efficiency and led to a massive reassessment of political ideas. The Holy Roman Empire ceased to exist, the multiplicity of states in Germany were re-assembled and the House of Hapsburg replaced its old title with that of the Emperor of Austria. The continued victories of Napoleon led to such an exaltation of the role of a martial hero that the age of Romance reverted to the concepts of the first heroic legends of the Franks and the Celts, of the Greeks and the Romans. And in painting, Napoleon was represented in the type of these romantic heroes and even his legitimist rivals were depicted in the same manner.

To confront the Napoleonic empire which replaced the multitude of republics set up on the French model in the surrounding countries, Europe was reduced to contemplating the necessity for a

War with France

(*Opposite*)
Napoleon as martial hero. This painting by Ingres recalls representations of Charlemagne.

When the United Kingdom of Great Britain and Ireland was set up on New Year's Day 1801, Gillray published this cartoon of alcoholic amity. O'Connell, more realistic, opposed the Union.

major re-organization such as had brought about the United States of America. The earliest practical emulation of this took place with the establishment of the United Kingdom of Great Britain and Ireland on 1 January 1801. The opposition to this move by Daniel O'Connell was at least in part precipitated by the growing militarism in Britain, which had been displayed at its worst in the savage stamping out of the rebellion of the United Irishmen in 1798. O'Connell was aware too that the forces of liberalism and of freedom in England were being subjected to extreme pressure as England increasingly feared the possibility of a French invasion of the British Isles. The history of much of this period so far as it concerns the activities of men like Grattan and O'Connell, as of Fox in England since the war with revolutionary France, remains shrouded in mystery. The renewal of public anxiety in the insurrection of Emmet maintained this fear of militarism, and one biographer of O'Connell at least has described Lord Norbury, who tried Emmet, as the Irish Judge Jeffreys. After 1803, the greatest necessity for Ireland as for Great Britain was the return of public confidence in a rule of law and order. It is not without significance that the Viceroy withdrew his patronage from the *History of the Rebellion* by Sir Richard Musgrave, in which that fanatic sought to represent the struggle in Wexford and elsewhere in predominantly Catholic areas with the lurid pen of a sensationalist depicting the horrors of the wars of religion.

British fear of Napoleon became such an obsession that Irish revolutionary nationalism, contaminated by its French association, was totally incapable of gaining any open support until after the final defeat of the French Emperor. In this context it is to be remembered that Robert Emmet, in his speech from the dock, showed extreme sensitivity at having been convicted as a traitor who conspired with the public enemy, France, and that his insistence that his epitaph should not be written until Ireland's freedom had been secured was partly dictated by his anxiety that his movement should be divorced from the public obloquy attached to the French connection.

It has frequently been stated that O'Connell was mistaken in putting the emancipation issue before that of repeal, but this view ignores the realities of public activity. O'Connell's only means of maintaining any national interest was by avoiding the militaristic position, which remained until the conclusion of the war with France. The cause of repeal raised as a movement during the war, once the Union had been enacted, would have been treated as an act of rebellion and O'Connell would hardly have escaped conviction of treason, with its consequences. The question of emancipation, then, enabled him to preach indirectly his nationalist views within the framework of a constitution which required to be reformed, as men increasingly admitted once Bonapartism and militarism receded into the past. In Ireland, however, the forces of law and order were able to

continue largely because popular movements could be represented as a challenge to government, justifying the frequent enactment of coercion measures and the replacement over large parts of the country of civil law by martial law. Thus O'Connell's nationalism was inevitably presented in the guise of justice for the King's Catholic subjects.

With no further need for an Irish parliament, the fine Houses of Parliament in College Green were handed over to the Bank of Ireland.

The Union and after

The Union between Great Britain and Ireland Act endeavoured to preserve the best interests of both islands. In parliament, to the House of Lords went a number of elected representative peers from Ireland. To the Commons, the Irish counties sent the customary number of members, and representatives of the more important parliamentary boroughs increased the Irish representation to more than one hundred. The financial balance between the two countries was maintained for some years, so that when an amalgamation of the exchequers took place the position of Ireland would not be adverse. The three Churches whose members constituted the overwhelming majority in the country were to be safeguarded. The Established Protestant episcopalian Church was amalgamated with the Church of England and the maintenance of this provision was declared to be fundamental to the Union. The Presbyterian Church, which had been, in the persons of some of its clergymen, the recipient of the *regium donum*, a royal gift originating with Charles II, was now endowed more generously. The Roman Catholic Church was provided for by a substantially increased grant for the national seminary at Maynooth, but in conse/quence of the King's scruples lest the admission of Catholics to membership of parliament would be a violation of his coronation oath, the understanding with the Irish Catholics was not honoured in this particular, a matter of such moment to Prime Minister Pitt that he resigned. This was, in the first generation of the new century, the most obvious defect in the constitution of the United Kingdom.

By contrast to what had been done a century earlier in the union between England and Scotland, there was failure to build up the monarchical sentiment in Ireland. The glory of Scotland in the eighteenth century had been associated with the maintenance of the capital Edinburgh as a royal city. Perhaps because of the rebellion of the United Irishmen, Dublin was stripped of its trappings as a capital, the Houses of Parliament in College Green being converted into a bank, the office of Chief Secretary being subordinated to the Home Secretary. Scotland had been able to preserve its independent legal system and had been able to ensure that few Englishmen would be appointed to public office. It was otherwise in Ireland, where the legal system was increasingly assimilated into that of England and the highest positions were reserved for nominees from the neighbouring island – and too often for persons of inferior calibre. Thus from the very beginning resentment existed in Dublin society at the down/grading which followed the Act of Union.

In the decade and a half between the Union and the battle of Waterloo, little of significance emerged in Ireland, except that with the support of old parliamentary friends like Henry Grattan, now a member of the United Kingdom parliament, the question of Catholic emancipation was again brought forward whenever the political situation appeared to justify it. As George III became more subject to recurrent fits of insanity, the favour of the Prince Regent seemed a possibility for those concerned with the Catholic interest. On the Continent in the conflicts between Napoleon and the papacy, English interests were protective towards successive harassed popes. The last of the House of Stuart, Henry Benedict, Cardinal Duke of York, known to a few devoted exiles as Henry IX, was pensioned by the British government; on his death the family records were given to the Prince Regent and are now the Stuart papers in Windsor Castle. At the Congress of Vienna, where the war was concluded after Waterloo, it was Castlereagh, one of the architects of the Union, who insisted that the Papal States should go back to the Pope and not be taken over by Austria. A grateful Pope only too readily co/operated with England on appointments of Catholic bishops, and Patrick Curtis's provision to Armagh as archbishop and primate of Ireland was partly due to his collaboration as Rector of Salamanca with the Duke of Wellington in the Peninsular campaign. Even further, the papacy entertained for some years favourably the idea that England

George IV, half a Stuart himself, contributed to the cost of this graceful monument in St Peter's, Rome, to the last of the House of Stuart: the Old Pretender and his sons Charles Edward and Henry, Cardinal Duke of York.

The Custom House as it was in the 1840s. It is still one of Dublin's finest buildings.

might endow the Catholic clergy in Ireland and that Rome might be prepared to accept a veto on its appointments there, if only to ensure that only loyal clergy would be promoted. Nor was there novelty in this in the Europe in which Protestant as well as Catholic princes were accorded the *ius patronatus*, the patron's privilege of nomination to the benefice in papal appointments to bishoprics.

The restoration of the monarchy of the Bourbons in France might be regarded as indicative of the participation of Church and State in public activities. The triumph of legitimism seemed to bury all recollection of the usurper Bonaparte, of the anti-religious excesses of the Revolution and of the incendiary slogan 'liberty, equality, fraternity'. At Vienna, the enthusiasm of the Russian Czar Alexander I for a Holy Alliance to maintain a concert, if not a union, of Europe was regarded as unreal and perhaps dangerous to the balance of power by Austria, by Prussia and by England, each proud of its part in the destruction of Napoleon. Moreover, with the end of the war, there re-emerged the spirit of liberalism which had suffered from the despotism of Napoleon quite as much as from his opponents, and among the liberals in many countries there were those who felt that it was not the kings but the nations that had arisen and ended the French tyranny.

O'Connell's duelling pistols.

Increasingly, after 1815, liberalism in Europe could rely on English support against the absolutist ideas of the Austrian Metternich. Constitutionalism almost inevitably gained Castlereagh's support and after him that of Canning in safeguarding public liberties in the restored or the new monarchies of Europe. Thus the united Netherlands, ruled by a Dutch monarch, proved precarious when it violated the constitutional liberties of the Belgians. Absolutist regimes in Spain, in Italy and far away in Greece under Turkey, were disliked, however ineffectively, by an English public opinion hostile to absolutism. Nationalism, when it was proclaimed to justify an independent Belgium and an independent Greece, secured liberal support when it was presented constitutionally and particularly on the model of the British monarchy, which had been limited by the constitutional instruments since 1689. If the united states of Europe receded from the public recollection it was in part due to the realization that the emerging nations deserved to be emancipated and that the spirit of liberalism feared more the image of a united Europe dominated by despotism.

Tory governments in the United Kingdom maintained for close on a decade and a half after Waterloo the principles of order and stability, conceding little to their critics and using their support by public opinion with much of the spirit of reaction that permeated the restored monarchy in France. Popular demonstrations of dissatis-faction with the political and social order in England were not frequent. They were handled firmly and in some cases ruthlessly, as in the case of Peterloo when troops fired on crowds which could hardly be regarded as riotous like those of the day of Lord George Gordon in 1780. Again, the savage sentences meted out to the Tolpuddle Martyrs, assembled to protest against social evil, links the establishment of the United Kingdom with those of reactionary Europe.

In the struggle for Catholic emancipation, O'Connell's great strength came from his knowledge of the law and his capacity to dominate legal proceedings, and through his successful defiance of the establishment, which he forced to rule in accordance with law and the constitution. O'Connell did not escape entirely as his methods of intimidation provoked government efforts to prosecute him or his supporters for breaches of public order. In the Magee case, O'Connell gained remarkable prestige for one of his greatest speeches in defence of a man charged with libelling the Viceroy. But while counsellor O'Connell utilized the occasion to defy the administration, his client went to prison and suffered financially as well as personally. Again, O'Connell was exposed to the risk of being shot in a duel, as many of his professional rivals maintained this old-fashioned custom of intimidating their intellectual superiors in legal argument. For calling the Dublin Corporation 'beggarly' O'Connell was challenged to a duel by D'Esterre, a member of the Corporation. O'Connell shot him

The duel with D'Esterre, 1815 – a rare abandonment of moral force.

dead and perhaps escaped the attention of many public bullies in consequence, though he did take up the attitude thereafter that he must decline any challenge on moral grounds. However, this did not exempt him from the charge of cowardice. As the Catholic relief question became more intimidating in the view of the forces of law and order, the legal acumen of O'Connell became increasingly involved and the emphasis on moral force more necessary to preserve him and his supporters from prosecution for incitement to public disorder whenever he held a meeting or acted outrageously in legal defence.

The writing of Irish history in the eighteenth century became influenced increasingly by controversial political issues in England, in America and in France. The history of England as written in the eighteenth century was largely influenced by the Whig interpretation of history. This thesis, elaborated in a book of that title by Sir Herbert Butterfield more than thirty years ago, serves to remind us that in the course of the last three centuries the eternal verities, politically, became identified with the struggle between king and parliament which had led to the deposition of Charles I, the flight of James II and the justification of the political events leading to the acceptance of William III and later of the Hanoverian dynasty as the orthodox interpretation of British history.

The fight for Catholic emancipation

In fact, as Butterfield has pointed out, the events resulting in the fall of the Stuarts were coloured by the assumptions of legal and constitutional historians that the parliamentary system had been in existence among the Anglo-Saxons before their invasion of Britain and before the beginnings of recorded history. The achievement by the Tudor sovereigns of their virtually absolute power had been partly brought about by an alliance against the Church of the legal profession and the well-to-do merchants which ultimately, in the seventeenth century, weakened the monarchy as against its allies, the lawyers and the merchants. In the process of asserting themselves against the monarchy these relied largely upon antiquarian lawyers who succeeded in transforming parliament into the key institution in the state. The legal profession customarily provided in court a system of challenge and response in which two parties contended with one another for the verdict of the court. This system tended frequently to dominate the minds of members of the professional classes in parliament so that a two-party system emerged in which all political questions came to be regarded from the viewpoint of one or other of the protagonists. In the eighteenth century, the views of the lawyers came increasingly to be accepted and when the American colonies rebelled against English parliamentary taxes and other regulations it was the lawyers in the New World who expressed the situation in continuity with the revolution of 1689.

It was this interpretation of history which was adopted in Ireland by lawyers in the parliamentary opposition like Flood and Grattan. It was this interpretation which created an increasing anti-English antipathy among the colonists in the period in which the Catholic population had been so drastically degraded that they were no longer feared by the Protestant Ascendancy. It has been said, not without some truth, that English governments gave more favour to measures of Catholic relief in Ireland when the assertiveness of the colonists against English administration was most intractable. At first, the leading exponents in Ireland of greater political liberty, such as Charles Lucas, were bitterly hostile to the Catholics and concerned themselves with reinforcing the restrictions upon them. From the late 1770s, however, Irish parliamentary advocates of constitutional liberties tended to be more favourable to the Catholics, whom some of them courted as potential allies against conservative government.

Not all the politically minded Catholics in Ireland were open to the advances of the parliamentarians. During the course of the eighteenth century, on the rare occasions that Catholics were permitted to express themselves collectively, it was in obsequious memorials of their loyalty to the Hanoverian King and to his Irish viceroys. These memorials were at first presented by the few remaining Catholic lords who had succeeded in surviving the successive confiscations of the previous centuries. After the abandonment of the exiled Stuarts by the papacy, some of the hierarchy identified themselves with such addresses to the King's representatives. A new situation, however, arose in the second decade of the reign of George III, when Catholic merchants of the towns organized resistance to proposals to impose additional taxes on them, proposals made at the instance of Protestant merchants jealous of their increasing wealth. The committee set up by the merchants became susceptible to influence from the advocates of parliamentary independence, though this at first was in a very limited way and neither the nobility nor the hierarchy showed themselves in any way sympathetic. Increasingly, it became apparent that the upper-class Catholics and the bishops relied more on the government than on the parliamentary patriots in their successive efforts to secure social and political privileges. As, however, the strength of the Irish Catholic Committee depended upon financial contributions coming from the merchant class, the question of parliamentary reform became of greater consequence to the Catholics. By the beginning of the 1780s, the latter had contributed financially to the organization of the volunteer corps who had begun to play some part in the movement for parliamentary reform, so that in turn the Volunteers expressed themselves in general terms as favourable to Catholic emancipation.

Edmund Burke. Though a Protestant himself, he had Catholic forebears and strong Catholic sympathies.

After the outbreak of the French Revolution, the anti-clerical forces, identified with the attack on the independence of the Catholic Church in France, accentuated political divisions in Ireland. The career of Edmund Burke is of some importance in this connection, as Burke, though a Protestant, was descended from Catholics only recently conformed, whose interests among his contemporaries were still a matter of concern to Burke. In the course of his closest association with the government of Ireland, early in the reign of George III, Burke had been seriously worried over evidence that in Munster the Protestant Ascendancy maintained their dominant position over the rising farming class by raising the cry of foreign treason to justify the maintenance of their social supremacy. The judicial murder of Father Nicholas Sheehy (executed on a trumped-up charge of being accessory to murder) was probably due to Protestant panic at underground agitation which threatened Tipperary landlords in the 1760s. Burke was concerned not merely to protect his Catholic relatives but also to encourage a conservative approach to the question of Catholic relief. He had been anxious to see published a philosophical history of Ireland which would get away from the polemics and the controversies of the seventeenth century and the stories of atrocities in the rebellion of 1641. In this he was disappointed, however, as successive writers on Irish history were less concerned with the philosophical approach.

The American War of Independence by its very success brought about new interpretations of Irish history in which the Whig view

A *Punch* cartoon of 1843 shows Mother Goose O'Connell dismayed (too late) at the killing of the Union goose. The golden eggs are labelled 'Rint' – a sneer from which *Punch* seldom refrained.

became increasingly evident. But while American republicanism had concentrated on the alleged tyrannical behaviour of the King, the tendency in Ireland was more concerned with the English people than with their sovereign. After the clear emergence of English commercial resentment towards Irish exports in the mid 1780s, Irish historical writing concentrated increasingly on the view that English influence was the bane of Irish development. In this connection it is to be noted that Daniel O'Connell, after the legislative Union, became increasingly critical of English rule in Ireland. The lawyer in him applied the methods of the law court and of the debating society to stealing from the revolutionaries their thunder against England. If, to Tone, the reform of Ireland depended upon the abrogation of English influence by securing the intervention of France, to O'Connell a repeal of the Union through the alliance of Catholics and Protestants could be secured by constitutionally denouncing English influence without resort to French intervention. It was in consequence of this that O'Connell employed the Whig interpretation of history to assert that England and not the Irish Protestants had broken the Treaty of Limerick by which William III had been able, by offering concessions, to terminate Catholic resistance in the southern towns. Similarly O'Connell used the Whig interpretation to argue that England, to secure the Union, had resorted to bribes and corruption to extinguish the liberties of the Irish Protestants, as well as Catholics.

O'Connell's attitude in this developed gradually and had little influence until after the abortive insurrection of Emmet. In those days, Catholic interests in Ireland were largely dominated by a grateful hierarchy, who appreciated the foundation of the Royal College of St Patrick at Maynooth as a national seminary under government patronage which would secure the country to a large extent from the atheistical, anti-religious and anti-British forces released by the French Revolution. In particular, John Thomas Troy, the Dominican archbishop of Dublin, utilized his prestige at Rome and his good relations with Dublin Castle to maintain good relations with the British government, even to the point of supporting the passage of the legislative Union.

After the Union, the King's refusal to accept Catholic emancipation virtually drove the Catholics into the camp of the Whigs. The King's friends, the Tories, were obliged, however reluctantly, to accept the royal view that to assent to a measure giving Catholics the right to be members of parliament was a breach of the royal coronation oath to uphold the Protestant faith. But the Whigs themselves were divided as long as the war situation existed, so that parliamentary reform was not really a political issue until after Waterloo. Catholic emancipation, however, increasingly came to be accepted as the issue on which Whigs could be united. When the Whigs took office, however briefly, the question of Catholic emancipation was again canvassed. Grattan and other advocates of emancipation believed that a government veto on higher appointments in the Catholic Church in the United Kingdom would insure the safeguarding of the Constitution. Such ideas secured substantial support among English Catholics and also from a few of the Irish bishops, but O'Connell was sufficiently influential to sway the majority opinion on the Irish Catholic Committee against the veto, despite the fact that the Court of Rome appeared favourable. Accordingly, the Whigs became tepid on the Catholic question. Perhaps when the King became hopelessly insane and the Regency gave the power to the future George IV a Tory government might have been found prepared, as Pitt had been, to meet the Catholic claim. Once again, Hanoverian prejudices were not to be overcome. The Prince Regent proved as bigoted a Protestant as his father had been. O'Connell threw his weight on to the side of

Silver button of the Repeal Association – motto, 'Ireland for the Irish'.

the Whigs, once it became apparent that nothing could be expected from the Tories. In consequence, with the revival by the Whigs of the question of parliamentary reform, O'Connell necessarily adopted their doctrines and preached the Whig interpretation of history.

O'Connell was not the first Irishman to present the national case against English government in a manner calculated to win external approval. In the sixteenth century, the Fitzgeralds of Kildare had represented their revolt from Henry VIII as a Catholic movement against the English heretic, in the hope that the Pope or the Emperor Charles V would support them. Shane O'Neill and Hugh O'Neill expressed themselves similarly in the reign of Elizabeth I, respectively hoping for French and Spanish, as well as papal assistance.

O'Connell was perhaps the first political tactician consciously to present the case he advocated in the framework in which his ally for the moment might operate. Thus his adhesion to the Whig reformers and consequent advocacy of emancipation as an aspect of parliamentary reform must always be seen as playing to the Whig gallery. As a piece of political manœuvring, this was propaganda for his cause concerned to strengthen him in building up his own movement, whatever that might be at the moment. Gradually he established such an ascendancy over his Catholic fellow-countrymen that they identified themselves politically with the Whigs to the exclusion of the Tories, and thus O'Connell's nationalism became founded in the Whig compromise with monarchy and the doctrine that Magna Carta, the Petition of Right and the Bill of Rights were the fundamental laws of the constitution. O'Connell, however, if he ever was theoretically a republican, had ceased to be so with his entry into alliance with the Whigs.

One can only hazard a guess as to the effect, fundamentally, on his character of O'Connell's victory in the emancipation struggle. In a speech in Ireland immediately after the Clare election, O'Connell announced that he proposed to attempt to take his seat at Westminster by openly defying the Speaker, representative only of a corrupt and rotten Commons against whom O'Connell would speak as the accredited leader of a resurgent people. By contrast, the case he presented at Westminster to justify his right to take his seat without subscribing the anti-Catholic declaration was a model of propriety. It was regarded as in the best of taste. It demonstrated admirably how O'Connell could attune himself to the mood of the meeting. It dispelled the current belief that the great agitator would be a failure in parliament. It established him straight away in the top rank of parliamentary speakers.

By contrast, the action of the Wellington-Peel government was in the worst traditions of British public life. The opportunity to concede the occasion gracefully was lost, both by the reactionary resolution to deprive of the franchise the forty-shilling freeholders, and by the

Medal commemorating O'Connell's election as MP for County Clare in 1828.

attempted humiliation of O'Connell, forcing him to go through re-election in Clare. Not surprisingly, it brought out the more deplorable aspects of O'Connell's character.

The speeches in public during the remaining months of the Tory administration were rabble-rousing incitements calculated to bring parliamentary institutions into disrepute. The personal attacks, in which not for the first time he indulged, outraged his English allies and stimulated the more irresponsible Irish Catholics to a degree of hysterical excitement in which they confidently expected O'Connell to lead them immediately to drive the English out of Ireland. Though he hardly mitigated his language against the Tories, O'Connell displayed his usual perception and applied himself to cool the people and restrain disorder, particularly in the agricultural community.

The revival of repeal was regarded by many as having precipitated this popular crisis. O'Connell's resilience is well illustrated by the manner in which he successfully subordinated this issue under the influence of middle-class Catholics, as well as of Whig reformers, in the programme he launched to justify his continuation of his movement after the achievement of its professed object, emancipation.

On the tithe issue, in the nation-wide Catholic reaction against being obliged to continue to pay this tax in support of the Protestant clergy, O'Connell demonstrated his remarkable powers over the people. It is true that there were outbreaks in a wide variety of places, so that government could only operate by calling in the military. But O'Connell, by systematic denunciation of agrarian agitation leading to violence and murder, established with the aid of the priests a moral hold on the people. Of course this had its consequences for his own character by giving him such a sense of his own power that it led him to maintain the language of revolutionary brinkmanship, realizing as he did that this strengthened him as nothing else did in the programme he put before him.

If ever a popular movement depended upon one man it was O'Connell's. Not surprisingly, it brought out in him the bully in dealing with cowardly opponents and timid colleagues. Not surprisingly, the moderate O'Connell who on such matters as the safeguards for emancipation had found himself in a minority in Irish meetings, gave way increasingly to the temptation to be less moderate in response to popular appeal. In his own character, it seems probable that in times of uncertainty, confronted by some great challenge, he oscillated between moderation and fanatical extreme. Whenever the forces of Britain appeared most adamant, most intransigent, he reverted to the cry that Ireland's injustices could only be remedied through repeal.

Outstanding among the Catholic bishops in the emancipation period had been James Warren Doyle, Bishop of Kildare and Leighlin, usually known as J.K.L. from his signature in public

James Warren Doyle: statue in Carlow Cathedral. Beside him kneels the sorrowing figure of Ireland. From his episcopal signature – 'James Kildare and Leighlin' – he was usually known as 'J.K.L.'.

45

Earl Grey, Whig Prime Minister.

pronouncements. Doyle had been particularly concerned with social questions, such as the appalling growth of poverty in Ireland in the population explosion. He had devoted himself to the education question and had proved a valuable influence in gaining support for inter-denominational schools, once it was made clear that the government was turning away from subsidizing proselytizing organizations like the Kildare Place Society. Bishop Doyle was one of the few Catholic bishops concerned to restrain O'Connell on repeal. He was well aware of the Liberator's remarkable powers over Doyle's own diocesan clergy. He counselled Whigs and Catholics to make every effort to win O'Connell away from repeal, to concentrate on the securing of justice for Ireland and the implementation of the Emancipation Act by administrative and judicial appointments to which the Wellington-Peel government and the Dublin Castle tradition were opposed. In the long run, frustrated almost as much by Earl Grey's government as by the Tories, O'Connell reverted to the popular cry of repeal, which gave him the emotional exaltation of the dictator.

O'Connell at sixty was perhaps more in need of a feeling of power, more concerned to restore his own tissues with the exhilaration of cowing his opponents. The attacks on Protestant statesmen were so outrageous to their co-religionists that a cold-war situation emerged in which Protestant Ireland, particularly in the north, rejected repeal. By the mere fact of nicknaming the English statesman 'Orange Peel', O'Connell permanently alienated both the statesman and the Orange Order, and in England he so severely damaged the Irish image that Thomas Moore, as great a giant in Irish literature as was O'Connell in politics, protested, setting down his rejection of O'Connell in verse:

> *The dream of those days when first I sung thee is o'er,*
> *Thy triumph hath stain'd the charm the sorrows then wore;*
> *And ev'n of the light which Hope once shed o'er thy chains,*
> *Alas, not a gleam to grace thy freedom remains.*
> *Say, is it that slavery sunk so deep in thy heart,*
> *That still the dark brand is there, though chainless thou art;*
> *And Freedom's sweet fruit, for which thy spirit long burn'd,*
> *Now, reaching at last thy lip, to ashes hath turn'd?*
> *Up Liberty's steep by Truth and Eloquence led,*
> *With eyes on her temple fix'd, how proud was thy tread!*
> *Ah, better thou ne'er had'st liv'd that summit to gain,*
> *Or died in the porch, than thus dishonour the fane.*

With Moore, we may well ask whether O'Connell's survival beyond the early 1830s was not more of an influence for harm than for good in the relations between Catholics and Protestants, between British nationalists and Irish nationalists. If the answer is in the affirmative, was this due to a serious deterioration in character? This question will be discussed later.

It has to be remembered that the achievement of Catholic emancipation in 1829 was the beginning of the revolutionary phase in the United Kingdom of the second revolutionary movement in Europe in a half-century. O'Connell, during the period since the legislative Union, had elevated himself to be the leader of the Irish Catholic organization formed to achieve equality before the law. It is also to be remembered that the Catholic question also existed as an issue in politics in England. So far as England is concerned, it was a minor matter. A small body of upper-class Catholics existed, very much under the influence of conservatism, very close in certain ways to the so-called gallican party which, in France, had upheld the privileges claimed by Louis XIV and his successors against the papacy before the revolution of 1789.

Beginning of the bloodless revolution

There was nothing of a popular movement about this question in England. There was little likelihood that any substantial body of Catholics would have been involved in England in the rise of the middle classes until the great migration from Ireland commenced in the late 1840s.

To a certain extent, O'Connell's organization of a Catholic Association, which gathered volume in the early 1820s, was an embarrassment to his aristocratic co-religionists. In England, an element existed among the Tories not unfavourable to the Catholics, just as an element not unfavourable to parliamentary reform existed among them until this question became a monopoly of the Whigs in opposition and Toryism slowly turned against any concessions to the Catholics. In the early nineteenth century, English philosophers like Jeremy Bentham were concerned to work out a practical basis for society and government in which the good of the many must be considered before the privileges of the few. The utilitarian principles of Bentham provided a convenient backdrop for an O'Connellite oratorical performance in England, concerned to present the Irish question as an irresistible element in the achievement of social justice. O'Connell was particularly remarkable in the English scene from his success in putting forward emancipation as a United Kingdom issue which few reformers could resist. Having regard to the Calvinistic prejudices against Roman Catholicism, O'Connell was particularly successful in winning admirers and even supporters among the Scots who felt particularly favourable to the liberation in England and in Ireland of the Catholics, as Presbyterians and other non-conformists stood to gain through the achievement of emancipation. It was thus that in the year before emancipation for the Catholics, the non-conformists of England and Ireland were given equality with the Scots by the repeal of the Test and Corporation Acts. These had excluded them from parliamentary and municipal office unless they conformed to Protestant episcopalian rites; the Scots had gained immunity at the Revolution of 1688. In these years, however, the position of Ireland changed radically so that the British Protestants came to associate O'Connell more with public intimidation than with public justice.

From the middle of the 1820s, the Catholic Association of Ireland, having become a nation-wide organization through O'Connell's scheme of mass membership with a subscription of a penny a month, had started to display an interest in parliamentary elections. In a sphere in which the landlord influence had been as predominant in Ireland as in Britain, so that compensation was paid to so-called patrons of borough seats in the reduction of parliamentary constituencies at the Union, O'Connell now successfully employed his influence to win the support of electors against their landlords. The O'Connell technique in courts of law, where Protestant traditions

were defied and judges and crown prosecutors alike were taught the
limits of the law and the capacity of a great Irish lawyer to intimidate,
now witnessed the same lawyer publicly indicting the parliamentary
candidates, defying the lightning that Tory ministers had so often
hurled at the cringing Celts. Slowly but remorselessly O'Connell
convinced the Catholic voters that their interests, their freedom,
depended on the rejection of every candidate hostile to emancipation,
of every theoretical emancipationist not prepared to oppose a government that denied the duty of giving parity to Catholics. Of necessity,
O'Connell's candidates who won the victories through the revolt of
the forty-shilling freeholders, as it has been called, were Protestants.
In Clare, however, in 1828, in opposition to Vesey Fitzgerald, a
Tory Cabinet member not opposed to emancipation, it was decided
that the Catholic O'Connell must himself confront the electors and
his overwhelming victory presented the government with the first
major demonstration that the conservative walls must come down and
that emancipation must be conceded to the Catholics in terms of
social justice and parliamentary reform. It was the beginning of the
bloodless revolution in England. It paralysed any possible English
opposition to the revolutions in France and in Belgium in 1830. It led
directly to the great Reform Bill of 1832 and established O'Connell
as an outstanding figure in British radicalism.

The achievement of Catholic emancipation made O'Connell one
of the best-known personalities in Europe. It was said of some German,
who was asked about Ireland, that his answer was that that was the

Repeal, decline and fall

49

Labels within illustration: KING DAN FOR EVER; DANS PARLIAMENT; BUTTER MILK; British Constitution; JUSTICE to IRELAND; NATIONAL; ROYAL PLUNDER CHEST No 37000

With a shillelagh for a sceptre and the British constitution for a footstool, King O'Connell accepts the fawning homage of his subjects.

country discovered by O'Connell, and of King George IV, who as King was as privately bigoted as any of his predecessors, that when he found himself faced with assenting to emancipation he complained: 'Wellington is King of England, O'Connell is King of Ireland, and I am only Dean of Windsor.' O'Connell, a vain man, was understandably proud to recount that in the deliberations to settle for a king for Belgium, his name had been put forward by several speakers. He seems also to have fancied himself as an alternative to Louis-Philippe when the latter became King of the French in 1830. Certainly O'Connell became an object of considerable interest to liberal French Catholics such as Lacordaire and Montalembert, as the man who had succeeded in combining Catholicism with liberalism, so that even Rome considered O'Connell above suspicion.

In the days after 1829, perhaps George IV was right and O'Connell was more of a figure in Ireland than in England. Certainly, he appears to have made an effort to initiate a new popular movement. He made advances to liberal Protestants like Boyton, a T.C.D. Fellow, and Sheehan, the editor of the *Dublin Mail*, with a view to exploring the

Part of a letter to Mary O'Connell from her 'ever doating' husband. His fluent, vivid style contrasts with her more practical approach (p. 23), but it is clear that their marriage was ideally happy, and that he depended on her greatly.

possibilities of a movement for the repeal of the Union. In spite of optimistic beginnings, Boyton and Sheehan soon abandoned the proposal but O'Connell persisted, travelling perhaps concurrently on parliamentary reform as well as on repeal, perhaps in the belief that he could still secure some Irish Protestant support, ultimately leading to power-sharing in Dublin Castle.

It is not easy to understand the workings of O'Connell's mind. Had he come to a crisis in his life in his fifty-fifth year? England had not accepted defeat gracefully. Sir Robert Peel, the Prime Minister, had little trouble in persuading parliament that O'Connell should not be admitted before being re-elected. Even the English Catholic upper class were at pains to ostracize him socially, and blackballed him when his name was put forward for membership of a London club. His wife complained that on visits to England she was not received in society. O'Connell, despite his boundless ambition, may at first have had doubts as to whether he could ever achieve in England the same remarkable, almost magical sway that he exerted at countless meetings in Ireland. Perhaps he saw the irony of the situation when the

Irish Catholic hierarchy published an address of thanksgiving for emancipation to the greatest living Irishman – Wellington. It is then understandable that in 1830 he should have again raised the question of repeal and followed it up with denunciations of successive British governments, Tory and Whig, for being responsible for Ireland's woes. It may have been good propaganda to coax the Irish Protestants into believing that he had no hostility for them. He probably felt they were not invincibly ignorant and could be converted to being led by him more easily than would the British.

Throughout his life O'Connell could oscillate between extremes – at one time the rationalist, at another, the victim of the most irrational superstitions. It was his colossal optimism which carried him in triumph to emancipation. It was the same optimism which led to his downfall in 1843, the year which he proclaimed would be repeal year. The pessimism after his rejection by English society in 1829 probably accounts for the decision to raise the question of repeal in the belief that his capacity to dominate Ireland was incontrovertible, even if he could never achieve a comparable dominance in British society. But this element in his character of pessimism, of withdrawal, would appear to have become accentuated after the death of his wife in 1836 and in the growing conviction that his own powers were greatest in the country, and in the county, of his origin.

It certainly took him some time to realize the strength of the alliance forged since emancipation by Henry Cooke between the Presbyterians and the episcopalian Church of Ireland. From Cooke's point of view, Protestantism was in danger. The rising generation of Irish Catholics were not to be trusted. Emancipation, theoretically justifiable, should not entail any power-sharing, any giving-away to the forces of sin, of Rome, of anti-Protestantism. As if to establish the correctness of Cooke's views in various parts of Ireland, Catholic rural communities after emancipation refused to pay tithes, the public tax levied for centuries for the support of the Established Church. While O'Connell was at pains to insist on the illegality of refusing to pay tithes, it was undeniable that, in his campaign for emancipation, he had sparked off the belief that victory would lead to an end of the oppression of the Protestant Ascendancy and of unpopular taxes such as tithes. Gradually, O'Connell was forced into the situation in which he again became leader of what was essentially an Irish Catholic movement. He enjoyed building up a political party in Ireland which included many Protestants, particularly among members of Parliament. He elaborated successfully a massive system of election activities which succeeded, if only temporarily in some instances, in defeating the landlord influence in boroughs and in counties. But in the process of raising political issues and winning elections, it was himself and what he stood for that affected the public mind, and to many Irish Protestants, particularly in Ulster, he was anathema, an ogre, as much

O'Connell's residence in Merrion Square, Dublin, still looks much the same as it did when curious bystanders gathered to watch the comings and goings of the great man.

To many Irish Protestants, O'Connell was an ogre. To *Punch* he was Frankenstein, raising the uncontrollable monster, 'Repale'.

to be feared as had been the Corsican ogre, Napoleon Bonaparte.

O'Connell, of course, could have retired from politics and it is possible that he would have done so, had he realized that in his person there was being created a divisive force which in less than a century would rend Ireland in two. It is unlikely, however, that O'Connell had any serious doubts about the necessity for remaining in public life. Was it not necessary to make sure that the Catholic Emancipation Act did not become a dead letter? In the long run, it was clear that Tory intransigence would be maintained, that parliamentary reform depended upon the Whigs, that Earl Grey, the Whig Prime Minister, required support to secure the passage of the great Reform Bill, and so O'Connell quickly rose to being an outstanding parliamentary figure, leading the ranks of the radicals, strengthening the uncertain courage of the government.

From this time dates the establishment in Ireland of a national system of education devised by Stanley, the Chief Secretary, based upon an undenominational principle, abandoning the demand of the Established Church that public education must be under its control. Stanley's plan might have succeeded, by educating together the children of all denominations, in terminating the mutual hatreds of Catholicism, Presbyterians and Protestantism. It had the support of O'Connell, and of the Catholic and Protestant archbishops of Dublin, Murray and Whately. It was not without some Presbyterian supporters. At first it had no Catholic critics. But the system was so eroded, first by the Presbyterians, then by some of the Catholics and episcopalians, that it ultimately became controlled by representatives of the three Churches, reorganizing the schools on a virtually denominational basis.

If O'Connell's help was given to the Whigs without qualification in times of crisis, he never omitted an opportunity to criticize them when their hearts failed them in Irish issues or when they feared the Tory taunt that they were slaves of the Irish King of the Beggars. The Irish Reform Bill, following that of England, exasperated O'Connell for its inadequacy. The failure of the Whigs to stand up to the Dublin Castle officials steeped in Orange bigotry, the public demonstrations of antipathy to the Irish statesman by the successive sovereigns, George IV and William IV, strengthened O'Connell's determination to maintain the policy of intimidating the English, both in government and opposition, to secure justice for Ireland. The question of justice for Ireland was no theoretical one. The Catholic clergy who had played such a part in strengthening the popular revolt from the landlords in the emancipation elections could now not be recovered except on terms approvable by the bishops. Justice for Ireland then became the clarion cry when repeal seemed likely to be an embarrassment to leading Catholics not prepared to believe that only through repeal could Ireland secure good government. Thus in the 1830s, O'Connell transformed himself so that repeal was subordinated to the exigencies of British politics and O'Connell's significance became greater in England than in his own country.

After the retirement of Grey and the succession as Prime Minister of Melbourne, O'Connell's importance was much greater, as the government was more dependent upon him. In 1834, William IV became so hostile to this situation that he actually dismissed Melbourne and sought to establish a Tory government under Wellington. The victor of Waterloo, however, was too experienced to acquiesce except in a temporary manner. But he induced Peel, absent from England on the Continent, to take over as Prime Minister though, as it turned out, it was but for a brief duration. O'Connell, with infinite patience and with that concern for minutiae which he frequently showed, organized the forces of opposition, worked out the questions upon which the defeat of Peel could be achieved and ultimately, in a series of private meetings, secured the return of

Edward Stanley, later Earl of Derby. While Chief Secretary in Ireland he planned a national system of non-denominational education which O'Connell supported, but it failed to last.

Sir Robert Peel – branded by a
hostile O'Connell as 'Orange Peel'.

Melbourne committed implicitly to securing justice for Ireland in
accordance with what came to be called the Lichfield House Compact.
So fearful were the Whigs of being branded publicly with being
dominated by O'Connell that Lord John Russell's biographer
Spencer Walpole denied the existence of any arrangement with
O'Connell. Nevertheless, from the return of the Whigs in 1835,
Melbourne saw to it that the government in Dublin would in
practice employ power-sharing, and a series of Irish measures to
redress Irish grievances were proposed in parliament.

In Dublin, the appointment of Thomas Drummond as Under-
Secretary ensured the observance of the new agreement and in the
day-to-day operation of activities Drummond won general respect
for his fairness and for his devotion to his arduous duties. The
government concerned itself with the increasingly menacing problem

Thomas Drummond, Under-
Secretary for Ireland from 1835 to his
death in 1840. He reminded the
landlords that 'property has its duties
as well as its rights'.

of Irish poverty following the population explosion which had taken
place before the end of the preceding century. And the more outrageous aspects of Protestant bigotry and intolerance were contained
even to the extent of inducing the reluctant William IV to outlaw the
Orange Order. As a gesture to this new dispensation, O'Connell
could not refuse to dissolve his own popular organization and,
perhaps inevitably, it created a crisis in his fortune. The O'Connell
tribute, the annual public subscription organized to compensate
him when, in 1829, he abandoned the legal practice which had
brought him the highest annual income of any lawyer, dwindled to a
negligible figure. Of his impecuniousness there is good evidence:
Professor O'Connell has assessed it in a recent article which expresses
the whole situation with the pessimistic disapproval of a trained
accountant. When, however, O'Connell was called King of the

Beggars, his critics agreed that he enjoyed a remarkable capacity to make money. They sneered at him because of the annual tribute; O'Connell answered that as he could earn ten thousand a year until he devoted himself to the affairs of his country, he was entitled to it. The question is more than an academic one, as there may have been something in the allegation, in the late 1830s, that his decision to remain in public life was activated by his desire to earn the tribute. O'Connell admitted to his friend and confidant Fitzpatrick his uncertainty as to the future. He retired to the Jesuit college of Clongowes Wood, where he undertook a religious retreat. Then he emerged, announcing that he should not abandon the Irish people, and he took steps once more to raise the flag of repeal.

Was he perhaps a professional politician, ready to dredge up the great question of repeal because it provided him with an easily earned income? Before attempting to answer this question, it has to be observed that contemporaries who insisted there would have been no repeal movement but for O'Connell were blinding themselves to the evidence, of which there was plenty among the Catholics of the professional classes, as well as among the Catholic workers discontented at the state of the country. Ireland had been largely impoverished in the Industrial Revolution, and this led the Irish increasingly to support repeal, particularly in a situation in which the British government continued to favour the Protestant ascendancy.

It became the contention of the Irish Liberator that the government had ceased to be effective. On issues relating to Ireland, they failed to contend with the House of Lords. Irish reform bills were so emasculated that they were hardly worth their enactment. Thus the tithe measures, first formulated to include appropriation clauses to devote surplus Church money to public questions like education, could only be passed by abandoning appropriation at the behest of Peel. The municipal reform measures, originally intended to democratize the boroughs, could not pass into law until they conformed to Peel's pattern which was calculated to exclude O'Connellites. If the Whigs set up an Irish Constabulary, it was only because of Peel's approval, and the police inevitably came to be known as Peelers. If a Poor Law for Ireland was enacted by the Whigs, it was with little support from O'Connell, whose concern for the liabilities of the landed class increased with his own pretensions and those of his relatives to be accepted among them. If the Famine which descended on Ireland in the mid-1840s revealed O'Connell's failure to evolve any economic programme, he gave little thanks to the Whigs for the legislative measure which put some limitation upon the appalling consequences of the destruction of the potato crop, upon which the great body of the poor Irish subsisted.

If O'Connell had in fact retired as the Whigs began to fall back before the aggressive counter-revolution policy of the Tories, he could

As Lord Mayor of Dublin in 1841–2 O'Connell was chief magistrate – which *Punch* saw as giving him an unfair lever in collecting the annual tribute from his followers.

The hostility between Peel and O'Connell which marked the last years of the Liberator's career is symbolized in a *Punch* cartoon. Peel-Sisyphus is condemned for ever to push the O'Connell stone uphill, and it continually rolls down to the bottom again.

'The darling little Queen' draws a parallel in this *Punch* cartoon between her rebellious Irish subjects and Tsar Nicholas I's even more rebellious Poles.

hardly have been unaware that, without his mighty power, the Catholics would have been totally unable to fend for themselves. In a certain sense, in his last days, O'Connell went through the tortures of frustration when his power had gone. It was then that he must have realized that, without him, the people were in danger of disappearing off the face of the earth.

It was in these circumstances, towards the end of the 1830s, that O'Connell established the Precursor Society, so called as a forerunner to repeal, as John the Baptist had been the precursor to the Messiah. Thus he began to re-organize his popular movement, which he was careful to represent in terms of loyalty to the throne and to William IV's successor, 'the darling little Queen'.

O'Connell was now in his sixties, a widower who had lost, with the death of his wife Mary, probably the most stabilizing influence on his career. When the question arose as to whether he would accept

Archbishop John MacHale of
Tuam, a father-figure to the Irish of
Connaught.

judicial office from the government if it were offered to him, his
decision was expressed that he must decline it in the recollection that
his dead love had implored him never to abandon the people of
Ireland. The loss of his wife, if only as a correspondent, materially
altered O'Connell and probably led him to become more self-
centred, more conservative, more attached to his Kerry origins, more
devoted to the Church.

As Melbourne's Whig government tottered to its fall, O'Connell
made every effort to revive repeal but failed to light up the country.
At the general election of 1840, his party gained fewer supporters
than at any time in the preceding decade. O'Connell sensed that
with the return of Peel his position at Westminster could become
insignificant. He decided to turn to the west. In the province of
Connacht, Archbishop John MacHale of Tuam had become a
father-figure for the people. Thousands of them walked for miles to

the Sunday ceremonies where he publicly discoursed upon their problems, their privations, the dangers of proselytism and the necessity of depending on their own efforts. To MacHale O'Connell turned after the failure of several Dublin meetings. The Archbishop, who had abandoned his former co-operation with the government and with his fellow archbishop Murray of Dublin, was prepared to sponsor public meetings in the west if O'Connell would abandon the Whigs as well as the Tories. Thus the repeal issue was raised under clerical auspices, after some preliminary heart-searchings by O'Connell. The meetings were so successful and so popular and so overwhelmingly well attended that O'Connell's opponents in derision stigmatized them as 'monster meetings'.

Coinciding with the return to power of Peel, *The Nation* newspaper was started in Dublin by a group of enthusiastic younger repealers under the editorship of Charles Gavan Duffy. Better known than Duffy to the next generation was Thomas Davis, leader writer of the paper, whose poetical compositions of a patriotic nature immediately lifted the paper above the dull level of contemporary Irish journalism. Duffy, Davis and their friend John Blake Dillon, of Roscommon farming stock, acted as a policy-making triumvirate and the paper, with O'Connell's approval, rapidly became the mouthpiece of the younger generation in the movement which came to be called the Young Irelanders. The name had first been applied rather sarcastically by an English writer, concerned to hold them up to ridicule as being only comparable to an ineffective group in the neighbouring island known as the Young Englanders. The *Nation* group, however, became much more significant in retrospect, partly because they were able to draw from the resources of O'Connellism and define it more particularly in the new revolutionary European nationalism of the 1840s. Mazzini had said of O'Connell and his claims for 'a nation once again in Ireland' that Irish nationalism had nothing constructive to offer, as it merely consisted of anti-English sentiments and grievances. Davis, Dillon and Duffy elaborated a multiplicity of evidence of Irish distinctiveness into doctrinaire statements, making the case for repeal more theoretical but also apparently more one of principle. As O'Connell mounted the repeal movement at the weekly meetings in Dublin in Conciliation Hall and at monster meetings throughout the country, he emphasized the necessity for an all-out concentration on securing repeal, postponing all other issues as utterly subordinate and insisting that the national effort necessitated consideration of immediately securing simple repeal of the Union and restoration of the Irish parliament. *The Nation* and the Young Irelanders kept the question of principle strictly in the foreground, not without some suspicion at least on the part of some of them that O'Connell would sneak back into a Whig alliance if he saw any chance of dishing the Tories and re-enacting the Lichfield House Compact.

Charles Gavan Duffy, editor of *The Nation* and a leader of the younger Repealers.

A weekly meeting of the Repeal Association.

Monster Repeal meeting at Tara in 1843 – rashly proclaimed by O'Connell as the year in which Repeal would be achieved. This meeting was said to have attracted nearly a million people.

O'Connell cheered through the Dublin streets in a triumphal car on his release from Richmond Jail.

Gradually, O'Connell was led to approve of a more militantly organized movement than in the past. Gradually he was whipped up to believe that victory was as certain as emancipation had been in 1828. In 1843 he proclaimed a Repeal Year. Victory, he announced, was certain within twelve months. In a series of monster meetings planned to evoke recollections of British brutality or of Irish glory, the old Liberator expressed more stridently his defiance of England and of her government. In October, outside Dublin at Clontarf, remembered in Irish tradition for the defeat of the Vikings by the Irish high-king Brian Boru, O'Connell was to hold the final meeting and sound the trumpeting note before which the walls of Dublin Castle would collapse. Peel banned the meeting. O'Connell acquiesced and called it off. Government-instituted proceedings against O'Connell and leading Repealers found them guilty of a breach of the Association Act of 1831 and they were sentenced to imprisonment, O'Connell going to Richmond Jail in Dublin where his treatment was more that of a visiting grandee than of a convict. Within a year he was released after the legal decision had been reversed by the House of Lords, where a Whig majority of the law lords were more partial to him than had been the packed Dublin jury.

O'Connell in middle age.

O'Connell's bedroom in Richmond Jail was in striking contrast to the usual convict's cell.

1843

**Estimated attendances
of over 100,000**

Sligo

Carrickmacross

Castlebar

Dundalk

Drogheda

Longford

Roscommon

Bellewstown

Clifden

Tuam *Mullingar* *Trim* *Tara*

Athlone

Galway

DUBLIN

Tullamore

The Curragh

Loughrea

Mountmellick

Baltinglass

Ennis

Nenagh

Kilkenny

Limerick *Cashel*

Enniscorthy

Rathkeale

Charleville

Lismore

Mallow

Waterford

Cork

Skibbereen

The monster repeal meetings of 1843
covered Ireland. The map shows
only those places where O'Connell
addressed 100,000 people or more.

So O'Connell was accorded a tumultuous reception. Archbishop
Murray even permitted a Te Deum and Thanksgiving in the Pro-
Cathedral, where in an impassioned sermon O'Connell's chaplain
Father Miley attributed his release to a miraculous intercession by
the Blessed Virgin Mary.

His imprisonment marks off O'Connell's subsequent movement
from the earlier phase. He had lost the will to fight. It was obvious in
his seventieth year that he had aged perceptibly. He became irritable
with the young men of principle, the advocates of more aggressive
pronouncements, and he took to task publicly more questionable
statements in *The Nation*.

The government of the United Kingdom under Sir Robert Peel
was a much more constructive one regarding Ireland than preceding

regimes. The Prime Minister, probably the greatest British statesman of that generation with the possible exception of O'Connell, set out to deal with the multiple grievances of the country. In an age in which the function of government was still largely regarded as concerned with the protection of property, Peel encouraged the deliberations of the Devon Commission which instituted a massive investigation of the deplorable state of agriculture and land tenure in Ireland. On the question of education, Peel planned to establish colleges to educate the middle class, mainly the Presbyterians and Catholics unlikely to feel drawn to Trinity College, which was still largely monopolized by Church of Ireland clergy and Protestant professionals. Peel also proposed substantially to increase Maynooth's endowment, to the satisfaction of many Catholic bishops like Archbishop Murray, though this led to the first divisions within Peel's party and to the resignation of the idealistic young Gladstone. O'Connell called in question yet a further measure of the Prime Minister, the Charitable Bequests Act, planned to facilitate Roman Catholic charities in danger of being diverted to Protestant uses, as English legal decisions had hitherto refused recognition to what were declared to be superstitious purposes. The unfairness, if not dishonesty, of O'Connell's allegations that Peel was preparing a new plan to control the Catholic clergy and convert them into government agents was to emerge half a century later, when Archbishop William

Prime Minister Peel is represented by *Punch* as a frustrated gardener. In his Irish hothouse, watered and manured, warmed by a generous grant to the Catholic seminary at Maynooth, nothing flourishes but the prickly plant Repeal.

The last portrait of the Liberator –
old, tired and dispirited – from a
sketch done just before he left for
Rome on his last journey.

Walsh of Dublin vindicated his predecessor Murray's favour for the
Peel project as against the O'Connell view, largely adopted over the
greater part of Catholic Ireland. On this matter and that of Peel's
colleges, O'Connell pressured the clergy relentlessly to secure
ecclesiastical condemnation of Peel and perhaps to strengthen his
renewed gestures to the Whigs as Peel weakened visibly before the
Tory revolt in the agricultural crisis which confronted both islands
in the autumn of 1845.

The return to power of the Whigs under Russell left O'Connell
with little of the power he had exerted in Melbourne's time. His
support was rarely needed but O'Connell lost no opportunity to
demonstrate his obsequious attachment to his old friends. Repeal
was quietly abandoned despite the protests of *The Nation*. O'Connell
need not have feared much opposition in Conciliation Hall but he
took no chances. The Young Irelanders, resentful at the attack on the
proposed undenominational colleges, provided an easy target when
O'Connell insisted on revising the rules of the Loyal National Repeal
organization. Henceforth there must be renunciation of violence; 'the
freedom of the nation was not worth the shedding of a drop of blood'.
Gone were the days when O'Connell had risked indictment for
sending his son to support Bolivar in the South American wars of

independence. The Young Irelanders dissented, arguing a little patronizingly that they were entitled to preserve a theoretical right to resist a tyrannical government. Davis was now dead, and they honoured his marching spirit too fervently to renounce the right of rebellion. One of their friends in Trinity, John Kells Ingram, had anonymously contributed to *The Nation* a poem in honour of the United Irishmen, directly aimed at O'Connell as impliedly a coward.

> *Who fears to speak of '98,*
> *Who blushes at the name,*
> *When cowards mocked the patriots' fate,*
> *Who hangs his head in shame?*
> *He's all a knave,*
> *Or half a slave,*
> *Who slights his country thus,*
> *But true men, like you men,*
> *Will fill your glass with us.*

Smith O'Brien, leader of the Young Irelanders: statue in O'Connell Street, Dublin.

Thus Young Ireland was driven out by O'Connell, who again felt free to re-engage himself with the Whigs. It was too late. The impact of the Famine on his beloved Kerry was so devastating that O'Connell could do nothing but represent to the government the urgent necessity of feeding the people. Ironically Peel's preparations at the onset of the Famine and for the first nine months of its duration proved far more effective than those attempted subsequently under Lord John Russell. O'Connell, who had been committed to the Whig support for the repeal of the Corn Laws while Sir Robert was still in office, could only mumble incoherently in parliament at the distressed state of his poor country. To those who saw or heard him he seemed but the ghost of his former self. Early in 1847 he set his affairs in order, though the doctors apparently thought him in no danger; he left Ireland for Rome and died on the way at Genoa on 15 May. In less than a year, the repeal movement had petered out in the abortive rebellion led by Smith O'Brien and a remnant of the Young Irelanders.

An attempt must now be made to answer the questions already posed as to whether O'Connell was more of an influence for harm than for good in the period after the achievement of emancipation, and as to whether or not there was a serious deterioration in his character. There is little doubt that in the attempt to secure justice for Ireland, O'Connell concerned himself with the problems of three provinces of Ireland rather than those of the industrial north-east geared to the industrial revolution in Great Britain. In the first instance, O'Connell was concerned radically to alter the conventions under which Ireland was administered by a combination of four elements, the Castle bureaucracy, the Protestant upper class, the British War Office and the professional classes. The O'Connell plan was to infiltrate the Castle, the army and the professions, and to force power-sharing upon the Protestant Ascendancy. There is no doubt that he successfully accomplished radical changes in personnel in the Castle. His influence with the army and the professions was handicapped as the number of Catholics with an adequate education for promotion remained small for another half-century. It might even be argued that had O'Connell won repeal it would have been necessary to utilize British and other administrators to train an Irish personnel. To a large extent, O'Connell's anxieties to secure equality of opportunity for Catholics made him so job-conscious that he exposed himself to the charge of corruption to secure positions for his supporters. 'The big beggarman' taunt was partly due to his constant appeals in personal cases to the Melbourne administration.

From the time that the Whigs under Earl Grey decided that the Irish Reform Bill was not to be as extensive as the English, O'Connell gave way to expressions of personal abuse which certainly influenced the less educated Irish Catholics into believing that nothing good was to be expected from the 'base, bloody and brutal' English. O'Connell realized that his offensive expressions against public men were the consequence of a defect of his character. On one occasion, he made reference to the fact that one of his sons, who had acquitted himself well in a controversy, should not imitate his father in abusing opponents. Yet O'Connell convinced himself that his methods paid off and that his ultimate success with Melbourne was due to having harried the government. The fact remains, however, that while he was substantially successful in his struggle for equality of opportunity in positions and in the impartial administration of Ireland, he felt frustrated, understandably, because in the 1830s the legislation to promote reform was dictated by Whig and Tory principles and because Ireland was increasingly administered by a bureaucracy trained to look at matters from the standpoint of capitalistic economists.

In the public speeches delivered by O'Connell on the Irish Reform Bill, on the tithe question, on municipal reform and on the Poor Law, he expressed himself forcefully and impressively with a wealth of factual detail, largely in condemnation of the ideas of British statesmen, and notably of Sir Robert Peel. It could be said that the tragedy of the Great Famine might have in part been avoided had O'Connell's proposals on the Whig legislative measures been listened to. On the question of poverty, for example, O'Connell proposed a state-aided emigration plan to transfer to Canada the rural workers for whom there was no adequate provision at home. Such proposals got scant sympathy from a legislature concerned primarily with the problems of British industry. When the mass

'The Real Potatò Blight of Ireland',
according to *Punch*, was O'Connell
himself with his collecting plate and
his domineering ways.

migration took place with the failure of the potato crop, there emerged
among the emigrants, particularly in the United States, such a hatred
of England because of their woes, because of the failure to such a large
extent to cope with the Famine, that Irish nationalism under emigrant
influence became largely identified with separatism. Was O'Connell
responsible for this?

To many Englishmen O'Connell was so responsible and in
recollection of his offensive and bullying exhibitions in public they
felt justified in denying to Irishmen the reforms brought about in
Britain. To Earl Grey, quite as much to Wellington as to Peel,
O'Connell was a dangerous person capable of bringing about another
rebellion if he could not be coerced. It was largely for this reason that

A contemporary lithograph shows an emigrant on Dublin quayside, studying the sailings to New York.

'Attack on a potato store', from the *Illustrated London News*. Looting and riots were a natural consequence of the days of famine.

the reform measures ultimately enacted for Ireland before the Famine were dictated by the need to prevent O'Connell from establishing a complete ascendancy over Ireland.

The decision of the Whigs to confirm the deprivation of the forty-shilling freeholders' franchise was bitterly resented by O'Connell. As he well knew, it was with the smallest proprietors that he had the greatest influence. Despite the loss of the forty-shilling freeholders, O'Connell successfully established a formidable party in parliament. With the forty-shilling vote he might perhaps have rendered government impossible with a minimal support of Irish MPs. What was not so obvious to Whigs and Tories was that the social and economic pattern in Ireland was being changed rapidly and adversely in the agricultural community by the measures of the 1830s and the early 1840s. Thus the forty-shilling freeholders, having lost their franchise, were increasingly subjected to eviction. The mass clearances which followed in many estates were deplored by O'Connell, partly because he realized that his involvement of the electors against their landlords had precipitated this. O'Connell was careful, however, to avoid whenever possible any attacks on landlord property; his attitude that the government should intervene by properly planned emigration put the responsibility squarely on the government and created in Ireland increasingly the feeling that the agricultural disaster was the fault of England.

In one sense O'Connell's statements on the agricultural situation might be regarded as prophetic in drawing attention to the serious consequences which could follow from the government's refusal to adopt his plans. Thus an absentee tax on landowners rarely visiting their Irish estates, so heavy as to compel them to sell out, might not have arrested the rot in Irish agriculture. But the statement of O'Connell proposing such a tax, presented with a multiplicity of evidence on numerous occasions, was ultimately to affect not the British, but the Irish nationalists. Similarly, his criticism of the Poor Law as likely to prove crushing to the Irish landed interest might seem prophetic, as a substantial number of landlords were bankrupted in the Famine when the Poor Rates involved them in unheard-of expenditure, coincident with the failure of so many tenants to pay their rents when the potatoes rotted. The decision of the government to impose an English Poor Law administrative system on Ireland certainly contributed to the collapse of the landlord system, as a multitude of bankrupt estates after the Famine passed into the hands of money-making corporations with little concern or knowledge of the older traditions.

Once again, it might be said that O'Connell's obsession with politics prevented him acting responsibly in the agricultural situation.

Funeral of famine victims: no money for coffins and little strength in the horse.

As an individual landlord, O'Connell was a humanitarian, who directed his agents in a cholera epidemic to sacrifice everything to save his tenants. Like many a Protestant evangelical, he seems to have regarded the plague as a manifestation of divine wrath, like the plagues which scourged the Egyptians in the Old Testament and which only the resort to prayer might allay. In this O'Connell seems no different to the economists whose remedy in a crisis when all else failed was *laissez-faire*. Would repeal have enabled Ireland to avoid the Famine?

O'Connell's obsession with politics committed him to the Whig government's economic principles, even to Peel's decision to repeal the Corn Laws. His public identification with Melbourne's govern-ment made it impossible for him except in general terms to work out a comprehensive policy of financing an alternative system of safeguarding Irish agriculture. And because he distrusted the Tories absolutely, he rejected the Tamworth Manifesto in which Peel publicly bound himself to maintain the 1832 Reform Act. O'Connell, in his hatred of Peel, foretold the doom of Ireland if the Tories returned to power.

Ironically the Peel government which O'Connell assisted in destroying in 1846 showed more capacity to stem the Irish Famine than would the Whigs who succeeded Peel. Certainly in his last days a deterioration in character had affected O'Connell's judgment. A younger, more resilient Irish leader, capable of objectively assessing the later Peel, would have known better than to drive out of office the greatest English statesman before Gladstone.

The historian, however, is in no position to come to a definitive conclusion in this matter. The ageing O'Connell, reverting increasingly to the Catholic traditions of his youth, to the attachments to the remaining feudal traditions of a landed proprietor in the poorest and most remote areas in Ireland, can well have felt that only through repeal could that Ireland be preserved from the cold, ruthless, in-flexible British interests represented by Sir Robert Peel. If the catastrophe of the Famine made nonsense of the O'Connell contention that the first priority was to achieve the restoration of the Irish parliament, it also exposed the incapacity of British statesmen to deal with such a disaster by expecting the poorest part of the United Kingdom to pay for the organization of relief with the collapse of the agricultural system.

To the day of his death, O'Connell was justified in his belief that he could restrain his people from revolution. If circumstances so incalculable as those which emerged in the Famine provoked a more violent outburst in the year after the death of the Liberator, the defects in his character had but a limited effect on that later develop-ment. If British nationalism, however, had little sympathy for Irish nationalism in the crisis of O'Connell's old age, it was indubitably

Famine relief, 1846 style. Peel's measures were more effective than O'Connell gave him credit for.

because O'Connell's public performances had materially contributed to the growing hostility in Britain to the Irish image.

The situation of the Protestants in the north of Ireland was one in which the reaction to O'Connell was not dissimilar to what he experienced in Britain, except that his transient successes in charming public audiences were not paralleled. Thus at Belfast in 1841, when he attended a public repeal function, he was subjected to insulting and threatening behaviour by Orangemen and by other admirers of Henry Cooke whose challenge to public debate O'Connell refused, terming him a boxing buffoon of a divine. Essentially O'Connell's northern audience was a Catholic one, but he did not let the occasion pass when challenged by Protestants as a member of a persecuting Church that had not stopped at the burning of heretics. O'Connell insisted that he had concerned himself with the promotion of unrestricted freedom of conscience and that he had always been an advocate of civil and religious liberties, all over the world. He certainly realized that his critics in Belfast did not accept him on this, and perhaps in this later period the occasions when he incited Catholic clergy to pressure their flocks or resist Roman efforts to moderate their support for repeal could be regarded as belying his protestations regarding freedom and liberty. It is unlikely, however, that he could have successfully preached the doctrine of moral force and the eschewing of violence to trade unionists, agricultural agitators and militant repealers without the support of the clergy, whom he continually reminded of their duty to advise on political and social questions, as he also reminded the Catholics in his audience to take no action without the approval of their priests. After his death, the clergy for a generation encountered no political leader who controlled them as had O'Connell.

In his last years, O'Connell, in declining health, must have regarded Peel's attitude on moral force as indicating a hatred of Irish political individuality. When the Tory Prime Minister announced the determination of the government, with the sovereign's approval, to regard repealers active with O'Connell as disloyal, O'Connell's answer was to stress the Catholic significance of his demands. Hysterically, the government's decision to increase substantially the army in Ireland appeared to some of O'Connell's episcopal supporters, and perhaps to himself, as indicative of an intention to use force against the people, as, allegedly, had been done in 1798. It was a tragic consequence of the extreme reaction of these repealers when O'Connell's declaration that repeal would be won in '43 proved wrong. In so far as this was based on reason it was because O'Connell believed that as in 1829 the government would have given way in fear of civil war. It seems never to have dawned on O'Connell, before the government banned the Clontarf meeting scheduled for October 1843, that Peel could have concluded that O'Connell was threatening rebellion. In the circumstances, the hysterical conclusion as to the government's reasons for filling Ireland with troops can only be attributed to O'Connell having lost control of the realities of the situation. Even though the state trial seemed to substantiate the vindictiveness of Peel's government, O'Connell's declared belief that the reversal of the verdict by the House of Lords was due to Providence would appear to suggest that he could never again command the movement as he had done before his imprisonment. Whether in fact O'Connell's powers declined, the note of hysteria was maintained and helped to infect the people with a hatred of England thereafter.

O'Connell, as a lawyer, had a clear awareness of the governing principle that not merely must justice be done but that it must be seen to be done. In his great moral force movement, O'Connell employed this governing principle to justify his condemnation of the Dublin trade-union combinations. If these were blamed for crimes of murder and assault by the employers, O'Connell condemned the workers for failing to make it evident that they were governed by the need to show

that justice was being done and not illegality. In the later repeal movement, O'Connell did not seem to realize that he had failed to prove to Peel that he was concerned that justice must be seen to be done. In consequence, Peel condemned him for inciting his followers to illegality, as O'Connell had condemned the Dublin worker.

After his release, O'Connell's mind remained clear but his powers in action slowed down substantially. He tended to see things more starkly as they concerned himself. He was particularly anxious to reinforce the House of Lords' verdict against his prosecutors, by treating Peel and his policy as malignantly directed against himself and all he stood for, including the Irish people. It is in this way that we may see O'Connell's condemnation of the Queen's Colleges scheme, really for sectarian reasons, and his absurd denunciation of the Charitable Bequests Act as if it were framed to enslave the Church. Perhaps his strictures on the Young Irelanders and on *The Nation* were in a different category, informed more by personal resentments against the militaristically-minded younger generation whose attempts to direct him had landed him into the ignominy of imprisonment.

It would perhaps be more correct to see his decision to alter the rules of the Loyal National Repeal Association, to outlaw violence, as an

The old leader and the militant Young Irelanders (represented by Smith O'Brien) are seen by the *Punch* cartoonist as the battling Kilkenny cats.

effort to protect the organization from any future stigma of conniving at rebellion than as a vindictive attempt to destroy Young Ireland. It has, of course, to be remembered that his ruthlessness in holding to his victorious position in the abortive negotiations for reconciliation left a permanent resentment on the characters of his critics, and notably on Duffy and Mitchel. This made them in turn incapable of appreciating his magisterial role in the movement and equally incapable of realizing their own incapacity to take O'Connell's place when they came, after his death, to write their memoirs.

O'Connell, like many another old man, may not have been effective in dealing with more than one main issue at a time. Certainly his effective re-organization of the Repeal Association enabled him to regain the confidence of the Whigs when it came to the defeat of the Tory Coercion Bill, introduced in the Irish crisis of 1846, after which Peel was driven out of office. It was perhaps his last major success in parliament. When he appeared there in February 1847, his mind still clearly saw the Irish situation more realistically than others. The tragedy to him was that the English did not see the magnitude of the Irish crisis, which could destroy a quarter of the population. With failing powers of communication, O'Connell seemed to sense the concurrent destruction of his Ireland and of himself. Ironically failing to achieve his final ambition to reach apostolic Rome before he died, his last moments at Genoa seemed to be bordering on despair. Was this in part due to the desolation of fear that he had failed his people by not maintaining better relations with England? It could have been small consolation to him that the Whigs, as well as the Tories, had not seen in the Great Famine the Irish crisis which was to disrupt the United Kingdom and partition Ireland.

It is difficult, in any brief account, to do justice to O'Connell. Among his followers, particularly among the Young Irelanders, the sense of their own abilities was sufficiently well developed to lead them to believe that they were comparable to the old man, particularly in contrasting their own activist views with his halting decisions after the banning of the Clontarf meeting. O'Connell often declared he was unconcerned with what history would think of him. Unlike him, the Young Irelanders appealed to posterity with a hotter gospel of nationality, and Irish nationalists applauded those of them who gave their lives for their principles. Thus, O'Connell was eclipsed.

It was to be O'Connell's achievement that the Catholic people of Ireland became identified with the principles advocated by Molyneux, by Swift and by Grattan, that government exists through a social contract with the people based upon fundamental rights. It was this political principle, as in America, which established the people as separate from the people of England. Before O'Connell, except for the few members of the Catholic upper class, none really shared with the Protestant Ascendancy the feeling for parliamentary liberties.

In the Irish parliament in 1780 Henry Grattan (to the right of the table) unfolds to a crowded House his thesis that 'the people of Ireland are of right an independent people'. But this meant the Protestant people.

To Henry Grattan's generation, the American claim that sovereignty was vested in the people was the basic justification for the demand for Irish parliamentary independence. But the members of the Irish parliament who won legislative independence in 1782 had very positive ideas as to who were the people of Ireland. They were the Protestant people. For most of them, only the Protestant episcopalians were the people of Ireland. Some of the parliamentarians might be prepared to regard the Presbyterians and other Protestant nonconformists as comprehended within the term 'the people'. Few or none of them thought of the Catholics in this way before the outbreak of the French Revolution. As the movement for Catholic emancipation gathered force, the opposition to giving Catholics the right to become members of parliament equally gathered force among the many Irish Protestants not prepared to change their concept of the people. In the argument for the Union, it was pointed out by long-sighted statesmen like John Fitzgibbon, Earl of Clare, that the Catholics would ultimately overwhelm the Protestant minority in Ireland and would take their power and property from them, if they were not prepared for the merger with Britain where there would always be an overwhelmingly Protestant majority who could protect them.

Before O'Connell's rise to power in the Catholic emancipation movement, its leaders had been divided between those who continued to put their trust in the King's ministers and those who preferred to court parliamentary nationalists like Grattan. The Catholic Committee was intimidated when the government passed the Convention Act to prevent any representative body being established which might rival and challenge parliament. The fear of the French Revolution, the establishment of a more despotic administration after leading Whigs joined Pitt in the War Coalition Cabinet, led the United Irishmen and some of their Catholic democratic friends towards revolution. It was O'Connell's policy after the abortive revolution of 1798 to regain public confidence in the national idea of Grattan and other opponents of the Union. After 1800, and particularly after Emmet, nationalism in Ireland virtually ceased to have more than a cultural significance for a generation. After the winning of Catholic emancipation, O'Connell revived the national idea in agitating for repeal of the Union. Essentially this was a demand to separate the people of Ireland from the British people in the United Kingdom. It was only those who supported O'Connell's repeal movement who accepted his idea that the people of Ireland had a right to be a nation once again. O'Connell's argument for the Irish nation was similar to the American advocates of independence from England and to Grattan's arguments in 1782. The social contract between government and the people involved mutual duties as well as rights. The English, O'Connell held, broke the contract by immorally bringing about the Union 'through bribery and fraud'. If O'Connell's view of the Union as being illegal turned out to be correct, the Irish parliament could be re-established by the sovereign so that political power would again be invested in the people through the King, Lords and Commons of Ireland. But O'Connell's people included few of those who in 1782 had regarded themselves as the people. The overwhelming majority of the Protestants and Presbyterians of Ireland declined to accept O'Connell's definition, preferring the protection of the Union as the people of the United Kingdom. O'Connell's definition was to remain the definition of Irish nationalists ever since, though few of them realized that they were in his tradition and that any movement for Irish political independence since O'Connell could have little appeal for those not in the Catholic tradition.

'Ossian receiving into Valhalla the generals of the Republic'. This heavily symbolic painting (note the eagle's lost tail feathers) by Girodet was bought by Napoleon.

The cultural heritage About the year 1760, the ancient Gaelic legend of Ossian, the saga of Fingal, the Highland hero of the third century known in Ireland as Fionn Mac Cumhail, first began to attract international interest in the centres of European culture. The Songs of Ossian first came to be known through the English poetic renderings of James Macpherson, an obscure Scottish schoolmaster who correctly gauged the interest of western Europe in stories of ancient heroes which he poured out successively in a series of publications. Translated into French, German and Italian, Ossian was acclaimed as the Homer of north/western Europe, whom Goethe was to immortalize in German literature. A school of painters stimulated by the ancient heroic tales utilized the themes from Macpherson's Ossian. Exponents of military valour became so drawn to him that the first Napoleon devoted part of his Malmaison collections to Ossianic paintings and throughout his military life was so attached to Macpherson's writings that he is alleged to have carried them in his knapsack.

To quote a later Scottish writer, 'The arrival of James Macpherson marks a great moment in the history of Celtic literature. It was the signal for a general resurrection. It would seem as if he sounded the trumpet, and the graves of ancient manuscripts were opened, the books were read, and the dead were judged out of the things that were written in them.'

The interest in ancient Celtic heroic literature did not begin with Macpherson. The English poet Thomas Gray had written of the Welsh bard. Others too had attempted modern interpretations, in Ireland as well as in Britain. Macpherson was the first to attract the changing literary fashion. And while, to the English under George III, there was little sympathy for things Scottish, particularly if dedicated to the unpopular Lord Bute, and to the Irish there was some belief that Macpherson had stolen their own heroes, the Scottish teacher's great achievement was to provide a prehistoric background for Celtic traditions as more sophisticated monarchical ones were about to be abandoned.

In Ireland as in Great Britain, the reaction against Macpherson tended to extend to his theme, so that only gradually did the saga of Ossian come to be regarded with anything like the respect which on the Continent led to the mingling of the Celts in the pantheons of heroes with Greeks and Teutons and Trojans. The American Revolution contributed powerfully to the destruction of monarchical dynastic legends and this process was to develop increasingly in France and in the Germanic and Mediterranean countries, where the worship of monarchy was to be replaced by republican concepts of liberty, equality, the rights of man and of social contracts between peoples and rulers.

In Ireland the Gaelic tradition had long ceased to interest the majority of politically minded people, who tended to look back to the traditions of England. The war which had terminated the rule of the Stuart king, James II, had resulted in many of the military-minded upper-class Jacobites going with him into exile and fighting under his standards, or as mercenaries in the armies of the European kings. By the middle of the eighteenth century, a few modest publications, notably those of Charles O'Conor of Balenagar, concerned themselves with the glories of Irish history before the Anglo-Norman invasion, in the same position as Geoffrey Keating had written his *History of Ireland* in the early seventeenth century.

O'Conor's work was treated with incredulity by Anglo-Irish historians like Thomas Leland, who had, however, sufficient reverence for O'Conor as a scholar to preface his three-volume *History of Ireland* (published in 1775) with an introductory statement based upon O'Conor on the organization of ancient Irish society. It was to O'Conor that later writers concerned with the Gaelic tradition were to turn, such as Sylvester O'Halloran, whose three-volume history would accord to the still surviving Gaelic families a historic background traceable over more than two thousand years. To O'Halloran, and after him to Thomas Moore, best known today for his *Irish*

Thomas Moore: portrait by John Jackson.

Melodies, who also wrote histories of Ireland and biographies of Irish heroes, the saga of Finn provided corroboration to his efforts to dignify ancient Irish tradition. Nevertheless, to contemporaries there was a degree of unreality in works of this genre until after the mid-nineteenth-century French savants and German scholars established scientifically that the Irish language was one of the oldest in Europe.

To Daniel O'Connell, the ancient stories of Ossian had little real significance, concerned as he was to lead his people out of the slavery to which they had been subjected. To O'Connell, this could only be achieved by a mastery of the language and the laws of the conquerors. Anglicization was a necessary concomitant of emancipation. O'Connell did not share the nostalgia of the exile for the lore of the distant native land. Rather, he regarded it as a valuable attribute and stated more than once his conviction that the Gaelic language was infinitely more mellifluous, infinitely more susceptible to the expression of subtle distinctions than was the language of the Anglo-Saxon. If O'Connell did not actively encourage professional studies in Irish to the exclusion of English, he unhesitatingly exploited every opportunity to link his movement with the attributes of ancient Irish traditions. With others, he associated himself in his later days as a patron of antiquarian organizations devoted to Irish history. The emphasis after his death on his indifference to Gaelic culture was much exaggerated and emanated largely from Gaelic League controversialists ignorant of their country's history.

Some Gaelic scholars who did not so condemn O'Connell have drawn attention to his interest in that culture. Had the philological revolution which established the antecedents of the Celtic languages in the Indo-European world taken place before O'Connell's time, he would hardly have failed to exploit, for his own purposes, the Ossianic legends. But he was not in any way an original thinker, except perhaps in matters of law and politics. O'Connell the leader was essentially a practical man. In his youth, as has been seen, his intellectual interests were extensive but he had little time for cultural interests, except in a general way to identify with his cause recollections and traditions recognizably Irish.

Perhaps the greatest Irish cultural interest in O'Connell's day was the poet Thomas Moore, whose renderings of songs and ballads made him the most popular literary figure in the United Kingdom in the first half of the nineteenth century. O'Connell, an avid reader of romantic literature, was much attached to Moore's melodies, which succeeded in translating to an English-speaking public a substantial body of Gaelic poetry. But Moore was more than the poetic genius who gave public dignity to an ancient tradition. He was also the gentle mourner of the dead who died for Ireland, and particularly of Robert Emmet. In the drawing-rooms of English society, the songs of Moore were sung and many a man who rejected the great agitator

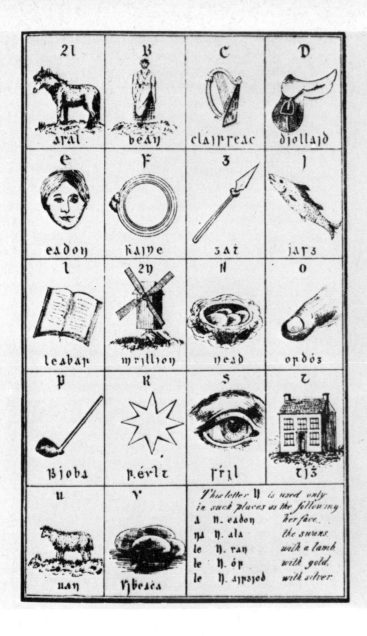

First page of an Irish primer published in 1838. O'Connell was not a Gaelic scholar, but he was sympathetic to the old culture.

O'Connell for his vulgarity and his turbulence gladly identified himself with the heroes remembered by Moore. While O'Connell, then, was rejected politically by Tories and Whigs on the issue of repeal, the nationalism of Moore secured the increasing acquiescence of Britain in the Irish cultural tradition.

About the middle of the nineteenth century the scientific investigation of the Celtic languages successfully established the bases of Gaelic culture so that the Ossianic movement, to which Macpherson's work had first directed international attention, became a matter of national pride in Ireland. It was this which led to the establishment in the new universities in Ireland, the Catholic university under the rule of John Henry Newman, as well as in the Queen's Colleges of Belfast, Cork and Galway, of chairs devoted to Celtic and particularly Gaelic literature and history. In a certain sense, this cultural movement became dominated by political considerations as the value of an individual culture became more evident in such nationalist movements as Fenianism and Home Rule. The fact that O'Connell was more concerned to emancipate the Irish people by making them articulate members of society capable of taking their place among the rulers of British culture, was forgotten by his successors. In the Gaelic League, established towards the end of the nineteenth century, O'Connell's impatience with Gaelic scholars not concerned in the education of the people for political life was represented as the rejection of the Gaelic tradition. In so far as O'Connell's priorities favoured anglicization as an essential part of Irish emancipation, he merely spoke as the articulate thinker for the ordinary people of the south and west. Thus O'Connell's rejection by modern nationalists involved their forgetting his sense of European culture.

In so far as the repeal movement led to the rejection of British values, politically it also contributed to the weakening of the European sense in Irish society. In the twentieth century, in which we know so much more of O'Connell's thoughts and writings, it would be easy to link him with the European cultural revival, once the repeal movement has been re-assessed in its historical context. In this connection, it is not without significance that modern American scholarship has become interested in the career of O'Connell as that of a great figure in European liberal and cultural development.

Ireland rejects O'Connellism   In the last months of his life, O'Connell became more and more obsessed with what he regarded as the inanities of Young Ireland and the futilities of Smith O'Brien. When the revolutions broke out in Europe in 1848, the Irish enterprises – scarcely worthy of the name of rebellion – were almost inevitably stigmatized as the Repealers' rebellion. In fact, such as it was, the insurrection can be described as that of the men who had rejected O'Connell, whose faithful followers, the Catholic clergy, had everywhere devoted themselves to frustrating the rebels. After O'Connell, nationalist Ireland could be divided into two parts. On one side was the clerical camp, which sought to secure itself by representing the dead leader as the devoted exponent of moral force, the liberal Catholic who had given himself all the days of his life to the struggle for faith and fatherland. As against them, theoretically republican, claiming association with the new French republic which expelled Louis-Philippe yet never absolutely affirming their renunciation of British monarchy, were the men who went into exile after being sentenced for treason or treason-felony, like Smith O'Brien, Mitchel and Dillon, but also including Gavan Duffy, who had been acquitted and who devoted most of the next decade and his newspaper *The Nation* to the cause of the tenant farmers. All this group, however, rejected O'Connell.

After the latter's decease at Genoa, his remains were accorded public funeral ceremonies in Italy and in Ireland. At Rome, Father Ventura, with papal acquiescence, gave a two-day sermon in honour of the venerated defender of Catholic liberties, whose heart was enshrined in the wall of the Irish college at Rome before the final funeral tribute at Glasnevin in Dublin, where the rest of his remains were finally entombed under the O'Connell monument, constructed in the likeness of an ancient Irish round tower.

In the year after the Smith O'Brien fiasco, James Fintan Lalor, advocate of the expropriation of the landlords in the name of the people (by which he meant tenant farmers like his father), made yet another rebellious gesture in which he totally rejected repeal. It can be said that the Famine disaster diverted public attention to the urgency of the social and agricultural crisis so successfully that the repeal doctrine was forgotten until it was disinterred by the new republicans, called Fenians, who first emerged about the year 1860.

O'Connell's attitude of hostility to government university plans did not prevent Lord John Russell from proceeding to set up in 1849 the Queen's University of Ireland with colleges at Belfast, Cork and Galway. He even sent Lord Minto, the Lord Privy Seal, secretly to

John Blake Dillon, joint founder of *The Nation*.

O'Connell's funeral procession in Dublin.

secure through diplomatic channels the approval of the papacy, failing to remember that similar intrigues earlier had only alienated bishops like MacHale. Despite its anxiety to be on good terms with the English government, the papacy was unable to approve Lord Minto's mission, as MacHale's success in securing the majority of the hierarchy against the colleges could not be unheeded. British intrigues were cut short when, despite mutual exchanges of information, the Vatican's re-establishment of the English Catholic hierarchy led to a public Protestant panic which the unstable government of Russell hypocritically condemned in the Ecclesiastical Titles Act, renewing penalties against Romanists using titles of bishoprics in the Queen's Dominions. The wave of sectarian riots, which the Prime Minister's gesture hardly contained, divided, significantly, for the first time Protestant Ulster from the rest of Ireland. In these conflicts, antipathy to the name of O'Connell was particularly marked and partly influenced nationalists interested in tenant right to deny their connection with the dead Liberator.

By the year 1860, the tenant movement had failed to preserve an independent Irish parliamentary party. Shortly before the American civil war, an Irish republican brotherhood had been started among American exiles, who modelled their political proposals on the American Constitution and on American antipathy to British royalty. It was in these circumstances that O'Connellism came to be rejected by those who accepted the republican idea. Not easily were the clerical nationalists subjugated. When the Pope was assailed in 1860 by Garibaldi and the Italian revolutionaries, Irish Catholic volunteers were organized in defence of the papal patrimony. Republican nationalists did not fail to express themselves sarcastically about the freedom of the Pope necessitating the shedding of blood. But the Irish expedition to Italy had considerable popularity, if little success. The papal party were not strong enough to crush popular sympathy for the Fenian movement, though it indubitably proved successful in defusing yet another revolt under James Stephens in 1865. Ten years later, under the influence of Cardinal Cullen, the centenary of O'Connell's birth was publicly celebrated and the foundation laid of another monument to the Liberator, erected some years later. Cullen, however, was unsuccessful in attempting to win popular support for what was virtually a Catholic party in opposition to the Home Rule movement led by Protestants like Isaac Butt. If the Home Rule movement, unlike repeal, presupposed a subordinate federal parliament, it rapidly came under Catholic influence, which played a material part in the destruction of the Protestant leader Charles Stewart Parnell, once Gladstone, the leading liberal, had become a convert to Home Rule. Thereafter, politically, O'Connellism was discredited, though the character of the Liberator continued to win admiration on occasion from such persons as Parnell and Gladstone.

Charles Stewart Parnell giving evidence to the Parliamentary Commission which cleared him of complicity in the assassination of Lord Frederick Cavendish. Behind him sits Archbishop William Walsh of Dublin.

The centenary of 1798 coincided with the rise of aggressive imperialism in the United Kingdom, which led quickly to the Boer War and a wave of militant Irish resentment of British misgovernment. From the beginning of the present century, the acceptance by liberals of Home Rule for Ireland brought about the re-organization as the Unionist party of Tories, Conservatives, Whigs and even Liberals. British industrial democracy was divided, partly out of sympathy for Protestant Ulster's fear that 'Home Rule means Rome Rule'. Unionism successfully manned the government of the United Kingdom for most of the twenty years ending in 1906. Irish nationalism sharply recoiled and asserted itself increasingly against British treachery in a language of revolution. Forty years earlier, a young historian, William Edward Hartpole Lecky, in his *Leaders of Public Opinion in Ireland*, had described O'Connell as the fourth of the great figures, after Swift, Flood and Grattan, who had shaped the expression of Irish nationalism. Now Lecky, a Unionist Member of Parliament, helped in the national rejection of those who advocated Irish self-government, who placed before him as their leaders the United Irishman Tone, the Young Irelanders Davis and Mitchel, as well as Fintan Lalor. O'Connell's rejection by the new nationalists seemed general after the survivors of the 1916 Rebellion secured endorsement in the 1918 election. This enabled them, though divided, to speak for the nationalist viewpoint when Ireland was split into two states in 1921.

Posthumously, O'Connell's contribution to his own legend was small in contrast to that of other remarkable men, like Napoleon. The French Emperor's memoirs, written in exile, played a powerful part in bringing another Napoleon back to his throne in France. Had O'Connell and not his less gifted biographers endeavoured to present his life, his career could well have been prophetically aimed at achieving the resurrection of O'Connellism. In the event, it was to be written in the pathetic vindications of his later career by clerically minded apologists like Cusack, by extreme nationalists concerned more to justify their own viewpoints like T. C. Luby, or by objective historians like Lecky whose admiration for O'Connell's constitutionalism was his condemnation in the eyes of the admirers of the martyrs of 1848, 1867 and 1916.

It is difficult to believe that O'Connell, controlling his own biography, could not have had a major influence on the thinking of subsequent generations.

Sharman Crawford in the 1840s, in a letter to Smith O'Brien, drew attention to the fact that O'Connell's nationalism had little attraction for Protestant liberals in the North. The romantic appeal to the glories of Ireland's past, the justification of self-government for Ireland which would recapture once more past golden ages were, he held, meaning-

Two states in Ireland

Sharman Crawford, MP, the voice of Ulster in opposition to Repeal.

Sir Edward Carson, whose slogans 'No surrender to Home Rule' and 'Ulster will fight and Ulster will be right' partitioned Ireland.

less to Protestant Ulster, whose traditions were closely linked with those of Scotland and with industrial Britain. It is in this context that one must think of the rejection of repeal in Belfast and elsewhere in Ulster. When O'Connell crossed the Boyne and went to the North he entered a world totally different to that he commanded in the remaining three provinces of Ireland. In the North he was the Catholic agitator, a term indeed employed about him by Protestants elsewhere, and even by some English Catholics. But in northern Ireland he was a faction leader who went in fear of his life. O'Connell was a man of remarkable moral courage but with an imagination which brought out the coward in him occasionally, as Grattan appears to have realized and as the critics in *The Nation* suspected over the Clontarf meeting. He was careful to avoid critical situations in his visits to Ulster, which were rare and usually confined to Catholic occasions when every security could be guaranteed.

It was seldom that Protestant pogroms took place in Belfast or elsewhere in the North in reaction to the repeal movement. There were of course half-legendary occasions, usually in celebrations of the twelfth of July, when clashes took place between Orangemen and papists. The song 'Dolly's Brae' recalls such an occasion but it is difficult to document it. Colonel Blacker of the Orange Order, a man who was proud of his Irish cultural interests and is even credited with a Gaelic ballad, was perhaps one of the most determined opponents of O'Connellism. He denied that disorders took place under official Orange aegis. The fact remains that popular Protestant protests recurred increasingly in the generation after O'Connell against public demonstrations of Irish Catholicism, against Fenianism, against Home Rule, and finally against the guerrilla warfare of the Irish Republican Army in 1919–22. Unionism was organized in the 1880s primarily to defeat the Parnellite Home Rule movement. Outside of Ulster protests, it had little significance until a gifted Dublin lawyer, Sir Edward Carson, took over the movement towards the end of the reign of Edward VII and by invoking O'Connell's tactics of moral force, brought the United Kingdom to the verge of civil war, which only the declaration of war on Germany on 4 August 1914 averted.

Carsonism must be considered as an analogous movement to that of O'Connell, utilizing a military technique to assert a great popular demonstration of solidarity against parliament, allegedly constitutional in its methods but employing the language of revolution to intimidate. Carsonism, like O'Connellism, had a limited appeal and few supported it outside of the sectarian traditions of the leader. When Carson on 28 September 1912 led Protestant Ulster to sign the Covenant against Home Rule, in which he was supported by the Moderator of the Presbyterian Church and the Protestant Bishop of Down and Connor, he confirmed the political divisions translated into law in the

Act for the Government of Ireland in 1920, which set up two separate states, Northern Ireland and what later became first the Irish Free State and then the Republic of Ireland.

The Carson movement had been primarily organized to frustrate Irish nationalism's concern to secure a parliament for Ireland. In this Carson failed and the compromise which established self-government for the six counties of Ulster, in which the Unionists outnumbered the nationalists 60–40, necessitated abandoning the Unionist minority in the twenty-six counties to make their own terms with the nationalist majority. Constitutionalism, as taught by O'Connell and practised by Parnell, suffered a setback when Redmond, the Irish parliamentary party leader, was rejected as having failed to win Home Rule for all Ireland. After Redmond, in an effort to hold his position for an undivided Ireland, appealed to the nationalists of military age to join the British Army and fight against Germany, the revolutionary nationalists gained sufficient support to proclaim their republic in Dublin at Easter 1916 after forcibly occupying strategic points in the

The Dublin General Post Office, stronghold of the revolutionary nationalists in the Easter Rising, 1916.

city. When their rebellion collapsed, the few surviving leaders of the Rising who had not been executed by the British were returned victoriously in a wave of popular reaction in their favour in the general election of 1918. Thereafter, the heroes of the revolution, Tone and Emmet, the Young Irelanders, the Fenians but not O'Connell, were evoked in justification of the cause of 'Ireland'. It took another half-century before that revolutionary tradition was challenged by many nationalists.

Looking back   During this survey of Daniel O'Connell and his world an attempt has been made to assess the historians who have treated of the subject, with conscious awareness of our great indebtedness to their work. It would be idle, however, to ignore the extent to which politics has dominated the thinking of those who have treated of Irish history. In the public activities in Ireland to the present generation, the popular movements in the Republic and Northern Ireland such as those of Eamon de Valera and of Ian Paisley have been powerfully sustained by an appeal to 'sacred historical tradition'.

Most of the writers on Irish history since O'Connell's day have been closely associated with politics. In the nationalist tradition, the most popular Irish history has been that of A. M. Sullivan, whose *New Ireland* was read throughout the United Kingdom in the generation before World War I. Sullivan was a journalist who succeeded Gavan Duffy as editor-proprietor of *The Nation.* If Sullivan was largely concerned with his own reputation – called in question by some Fenians – he was at one with his critics in denigrating O'Connell, and in attributing to Young Ireland the credit for reviving Irish nationalism when it had sunk into oblivion with the fall of the United Irishmen. Among contemporaries of Sullivan writing on Irish history were Mitchel and Luby, John O'Leary and the forger Piggott, all practised professional journalists, all concerned to exploit history in pursuit of their own propaganda. Not until after the Irish self-government Acts of 1921–2 was this situation to be regarded differently. Yet O'Connell, because of his Catholic associations, remained such a controversial figure, and to many Irish Protestants such a malevolent one, that it is only in the middle of the present century, with the publication of *Nine Centenary Essays* edited by Michael Tierney, that O'Connell's career began to be assessed in an objective historical manner.

Perhaps in the not far distant future, the career of O'Connell will re-emerge as of great significance to historians as part of the great European tradition, on both sides of the Atlantic, which began to be lighted up when Edmund Burke wrote his first philosophical disquisitions on behalf of the Irish Catholics and the American colonists. In the history of that chapter in the development of European civilization, the name of Daniel O'Connell may be remembered as that of a great political leader whose achievements outweigh his great deficiencies.

Among the remarkable characters of history O'Connell will stand out as one of the greatest organizers of mass movements. If he failed to build up a political machine to continue in existence in subsequent generations, it was perhaps the consequence of his concentration on repeal, which became increasingly irrelevant in an Ireland gripped by Famine, and in 1848 with the attempted rising of the Young Irelanders. The only characters in modern Irish political history who compare with him are Parnell and de Valera.

The Liberator looks down at the street which bears his name.

BLACKER, WILLIAM (1777–1855)
Soldier and song-writer. B.A. Trinity
College, Dublin 1799. Witnessed
Diamond fight and subsequently
became a member of the Orange
Order. Joined 60th Regiment and
became Colonel. Published *Armagh*
in 1848.

BOYTON, CHARLES (1799–1844)
B.A. Trinity College, Dublin 1819.
Fellow 1821. D.D. 1838. Leading
spirit in Irish Protestant Conservative Society. In 1836 he accepted
living in Donegal and ceased to play
an active part in politics.

BURKE, EDMUND (1729–97) B.A.
Trinity College, Dublin 1748. Ac-
companied William Hamilton to
Ireland 1761–2, 1763–4. MP 1765.
Opposed to government's American
policy. Wrote *Some Thoughts on
Present Discontents* in 1770. Kept out
of office when Whigs came into
power in 1782. Urged self-
government for Ireland in 1782.
Strong supporter of Catholic emancipation. Active in impeaching Warren
Hastings. Supported Fox in Regency
crisis. *Reflections* published in 1790.
Broke with Fox and Whigs in 1791.
Opposed to relief for Unitarians and
to parliamentary reform 1792. Retired from parliament 1792. Encouraged foundation of Maynooth.
Letters on a Regicide Peace published in
1796.

BUTT, ISAAC (1813–79) LL.D.
Trinity College, Dublin 1840. Edited
Dublin University Magazine 1843–8.
Professor of political economy 1836–
41. Opposed to O'Connell. MP
1852. Defended Fenian prisoners
1865–9. Founder of Home Rule
party.

CARSON, SIR EDWARD (1854–1935)
Educated at Trinity College, Dublin.
Notable barrister. Led Unionist op-
position to Home Rule 1905–15.
Brought about Covenant of 1912.

COOKE, HENRY (1788–1868) Studied
at Glasgow and at Dublin 1815–18.
Presbyterian minister 1808. Professor of sacred rhetoric and cate-
chetics at Assembly College, Belfast
1847. Leader of orthodox movement which excluded Arian ministers
from Presbyterian Church. Strongly
opposed to disestablishment of
Church. One of the most effective
preachers and debaters of his day.

CRAWFORD, WILLIAM SHARMAN
(1781–1861) Sheriff of Down 1811.
Advocate of Catholic emancipation.
MP 1835–7, 1841–52. Brought forward Bill to compensate evicted
tenants, which was defeated in 1835.
Supporter of Chartists. Instrumental in establishing Tenant Right in
Ulster 1846. Promulgated federal
scheme in opposition to O'Connell
in 1843.

CULLEN, PAUL (1803–78) Studied at Carlow College and in Rome. Made a doctor by the Pope 1828. Rector of Irish College in Rome and of Propaganda College 1848–9, which he saved from Mazzini by placing under American protection. Archbishop of Armagh 1849–52. Archbishop of Dublin 1852. Delegate apostolic to Catholic university in Ireland. Opposed to Fenians. Made a cardinal 1866.

CURTIS, PATRICK (1740–1832) Professor of astronomy and natural history at Salamanca. Arrested as a spy by French in 1811. Returned to Ireland 1818. Archbishop of Armagh 1819. Advocated Catholic emancipation before House of Lords Committee in 1825. Had correspondence with Wellington.

DAVIS, THOMAS (1814–45) Graduated from Trinity College, Dublin 1836. Called to Bar in 1838. In association with Duffy and Dillon, founded The Nation, to which he contributed many poems and ballads. Broke away from O'Connell to found Young Ireland party in 1845, but later reconciled.

DILLON, JOHN BLAKE (1816–66) Graduate and moderator, Trinity College, Dublin. Called to Irish Bar in 1841. Joint founder of The Nation. Led rebels at Mullinahone and Killenaune in 1848. Escaped to America.

DOYLE, JAMES WARREN (1786–1834) Augustinian monk 1806. Entered university of Coimbra. Volunteer under Wellesley in Spain. Bishop of Kildare and Leighlin 1819. Reformed discipline of his diocese and attacked established Church. Examined by parliamentary committees on state of Ireland 1825, 1830 and 1832. Built cathedral at Carlow and published Letters on the State of Ireland in 1824 and 1825.

DRUMMOND, THOMAS (1797–1840) Entered Royal Engineers in 1815. Under-Secretary at Dublin Castle 1835–40. Initiated programme of reform. 'Property has its duties as well as its rights,' he told Irish landlords. Supported by O'Connell. His administration vindicated by a commission of inquiry.

DUFFY, CHARLES GAVAN (1816–1903) Became a journalist in Dublin 1836. Started The Nation as proprietor and editor in 1842. Brought out 'Library of Ireland'. Accused with O'Connell of sedition in 1844. Opposed to federalism. Called to Irish Bar in 1845. Became intimate with Carlyle 1845. Formed Irish Confederation in 1847. Suggested formation of independent Irish party at Westminster 1848. Arrested and The Nation suppressed 1848–9. Joined Tenant League in 1852. Emigrated to Australia 1855.

EMMET, ROBERT (1778–1803) Entered Trinity College, Dublin 1793. Visited Paris and saw Napoleon and Talleyrand in 1802. Planned rising in 1803. Lost heart at violence of followers. Arrested, tried and executed 1803.

FITZGERALD, MAURICE, KNIGHT OF KERRY (1774–1849) Represented Kerry for thirty-seven years in Irish and imperial parliaments. Commissioner for Customs in Ireland 1799–1802. Lord of the Treasury 1827. Vice-treasurer of Ireland 1830. Unable to regain his seat for Kerry after Reform Act. Friend of Wellington and Castlereagh.

FITZGERALD, WILLIAM VESEY, later Baron Fitzgerald and Vesey. MP 1808. Irish privy councillor 1810. English privy councillor 1812. Chancellor of Irish Exchequer 1812–16. MP Clare 1818. Paymaster-General 1826. President of Board of Trade

1828. Defeated by O'Connell 1828. President of Board of Control 1841–3.

FITZPATRICK, PATRICK VINCENT (1792–1865) Friend and confidant of O'Connell, for whom he collected 'the Rent' for many years. Appointed Registrar of Deeds through O'Connell's influence.

FLOOD, HENRY (1732–91) Natural son of Chief Justice Warden Flood. Entered Irish parliament for Kilkenny 1759. Carried rejection of Money Bill 1769. Vice-treasurer of Ireland 1775. Colonel in Volunteers. Co-operated with Grattan in obtaining the legislative independence of the Irish parliament 1782. Quarrelled with Grattan on retention of Volunteers and on Catholic relief. Introduced several reform bills.

GORDON, LORD GEORGE (1751–93) MP 1774–81. President of Protestant Association for repeal of Relief Act of 1778. Presented petition which led to riots in 1780. Acquitted of treason 1781. Died in Newgate.

GRATTAN, HENRY (1746–1820) Graduated from Trinity College, Dublin 1767. With Flood contributed articles to *Freeman's Journal*. Played a large part in gaining of legislative independence for Irish parliament 1782. Seceded from House after rejection of Ponsonby's reforms. Spoke against Union. MP for Dublin 1806–20. Declined office. Raised question of Catholic emancipation in 1813 and introduced Bill.

KEATING, GEOFFREY (1570?–1644) Author of *Foras Feasa ar Eirinn* which was widely circulated in MS.

KENMARE, 4TH VISCOUNT, Sir Thomas Browne (1726–95) Active in Catholic Committee. One of the largest Catholic landowners in Ireland. Wyse wrote of him: 'Cold, unconciliating, timid, yet fond of petty power, hanging between Catholic and Protestant'.

KEOGH, JOHN (1740–1817) Irish Catholic leader. Instrumental in bringing about Irish Catholic Relief Act of 1793. Arrested as member of United Irishmen in 1796. Released and withdrew from public affairs after 1798, but was associated with O'Connell and the Catholic Committee.

KILWARDEN, LORD, Arthur Wolfe (1739–1803) B.A. Trinity College, Dublin 1760. Solicitor-General 1787. Attorney-General and privy councillor 1789. Appointed Chief Justice 1798. Murdered by rebels during Emmet's insurrection.

LALOR, JAMES FINTAN (1807–49) Contributed to *The Nation* 1847. Prominent in revolutionary circles 1847–8. Edited *The Irish Felon* in 1848.

LELAND, THOMAS (1722–85) Entered Trinity College, Dublin 1737. Vicar of St Anne's in Dublin. Published *History of Ireland from the invasion of Henry II, with a preliminary Discourse on the ancient state of that Kingdom* 1773.

LUCAS, CHARLES (1713–71) 'The Wilkes of Ireland'. Interested himself in municipal reform in Ireland and published *An Apology for the Civil Rights and Liberties of the Commons and Citizens of Dublin* 1774. Outlawed in 1748. Studied medicine at Paris and Leyden. MP Dublin 1761–71. Contributor to *Freeman's Journal*.

MACHALE, JOHN (1791–1881) Educated at Maynooth. Lecturer on

theology there 1814. Coadjutor bishop of Killala 1825. Archbishop of Tuam 1834. 'Induced by his dislike of everything English to oppose Newman' (*DNB*). Quarrelled with Cullen. Translated some of Moore's 'Melodies' into Irish.

MACPHERSON, JAMES (1736–96) Studied at Aberdeen and Edinburgh. Published *The Highlander* 1758; *Fingal* 1762; *Fragments of Ancient Poetry collected in the Highlands* 1760; *Temora* 1763. Attacked by Johnson in his *Journey to the Western Isles* 1766. Employed by North's ministry to defend their American policy. In 1797, after Macpherson's death, the Highland Society investigated the Ossianic poems. 'They reported that while a great legend of Fingal and Ossian existed in Scotland, Macpherson had liberally edited his originals and inserted passages of his own. Subsequent investigation has confirmed the committee's conclusions' (*DNB*).

MILEY, FR. JOHN Educated at Maynooth and Rome. Attempted to reconcile O'Connell and Young Irelanders in 1846. Went with O'Connell to Italy in 1847. Rector of the Irish College in Rome 1849–59.

MINTO, 2ND EARL OF, Gilbert Elliot (1782–1859) Educated at Edinburgh University. Whig MP 1806–14. British Ambassador to Berlin 1832–4. First Lord of the Admiralty 1835–41. Lord Privy Seal 1846.

MITCHEL, JOHN (1815–75) Matriculated at Trinity College, Dublin 1830. Solicitor 1840. Supporter of Repeal Association 1843–6. On staff of *The Nation* 1845–7. Started *Weekly Irishman* 1848. Tried for sedition and transported 1848. Escaped to San Francisco 1853. Later elected MP.

MOLYNEUX, WILLIAM (1656–98) Brother of Sir Thomas Molyneux. Entered Middle Temple in 1675. Surveyor-General of the King's buildings 1684–8. FRS 1685. Commissioner for army accounts 1690. MP Dublin University 1692 and 1695. Best known for *Case of Ireland . . . stated* 1698.

MURREY, DANIEL (1768–1852) Studied at Dublin and Salamanca. Coadjutor to Archbishop of Dublin 1809. Succeeded to see 1823. Corresponded with Newman.

MUSGRAVE, SIR RICHARD (1757?–1818) MP 1778. Wrote on contemporary political events. Attached to English connection but opposed to Union.

NORBURY, 1ST EARL OF, John Toler (1745–1831) Called to Irish Bar 1770. MP 1776. Opposed Flood's reform bill 1783. Solicitor-General 1789. Opposed Grattan on sale of peerages and honours. Consistent supporter of Westmorland and Camden. Moved rejection of relief bill 1795. Ruthlessly suppressed rebellion in 1798. Chief Justice of the Common Pleas 1800. One of the chief supporters of the Ascendancy.

O'BRIEN, WILLIAM SMITH (1803–64) Educated at Harrow and Trinity College, Cambridge. MP 1823–31. Supporter of Peel and Catholic emancipation. Introduced Irish Poor Law Bill. Made repeated efforts to improve poor law relief in Ireland. Joined Repeal Association 1843. Broke away and founded Irish Confederation 1846. Urged formation of national guard for Ireland 1848. Tried to raise rebellion but was sentenced to death; sentence commuted to transportation. Pardoned 1854.

O'CONNELL, DANIEL CHARLES, COUNT (1745–1833) Entered French army in 1760. Became adjutant of Clare regiment. Obtained cross of St Louis for a pamphlet on army discipline. Supported Revolution at first but joined Bourbons in 1792 in exile. Suggested formation of an Irish regiment to Pitt 1796. Became a lieutenant-general at restoration. Died at Madon in Blois.

O'CONNELL, MARY (1778–1836) Cousin of O'Connell. Married him secretly on 23 June 1802. Died October 1836.

O'CONNELL, MAURICE 'HUNTING CAP' (1726–1825) Deputy Governor of Kerry 1793. Owner of Derrynane Abbey which he left to his nephew, Daniel. He also left some £54,000 in other assets. A considerable landowner.

O'CONOR, CHARLES (1710–91) Irish antiquary. Published *Dissertations on the Ancient History of Ireland* 1753. Collected Irish MSS. and published pamphlets on the abolition of political disabilities of Roman Catholics.

O'HALLORAN, SYLVESTER (1728–1807) Surgeon and antiquary. Studied at Paris and Leyden. Published, in 1774, *Ierne Defended* and also *General History of Ireland to the close of the twelfth century*.

PARNELL, CHARLES STEWART (1846–91) MP 1875. Chairman of Home Rule Party in House of Commons 1880. His agitation brought about Land Act of 1881. Supported Home Rule Bill of 1886. Lost leadership of Irish party after O'Shea divorce case.

PARNELL, SIR HENRY (1776–1842) MP Irish House of Commons 1797 and imperial parliament 1802. Not-able supporter of Catholic emancipation from 1810. Secretary for War in Grey's administration. Treasurer of the Navy under Melbourne 1835, and Paymaster-General 1836–42. Had a high reputation as a political economist.

PONSONBY, GEORGE (1755–1817) MP Irish parliament 1776–1800. Chancellor of Exchequer under Portland 1782. Supported emancipation and left political life when unable to obtain Catholic relief. Opposed Union. Lord Chancellor of Ireland 1806. Leader of opposition from 1808.

PONSONBY, JOHN WILLIAM, 4th Earl of Bessborough (1781–1847) Home Secretary under Melbourne 1834–5. Lord Lieutenant of Ireland 1846–7.

PORTLAND, 3RD DUKE OF, William Henry Cavendish Bentinck (1738–1809) Lord Lieutenant of Ireland 1782. Prime Minister 1783. Allied with Pitt at time of French Revolution. Home Secretary 1794–1801. Greatly assisted passing of Union. Lord President of Council in Addington's and Pitt's cabinets. Prime Minister 1807. Resigned 1809.

SHEEHAN, REMIGIUS Cork attorney. Became editor of *Dublin Evening Mail* in 1824. Became proprietor of newspaper *Star of Brunswick c.* 1828 in order to combat emancipation movement. His brother Thomas was joint proprietor of *Dublin Evening Mail*. Given freedom of Dublin in 1828.

SHEEHY, FR. NICHOLAS (1728–66) Executed on charge of complicity in murder of informer Bridges.

STANLEY, EDWARD (1799–1869) 14th Earl of Derby. Irish Secretary 1830–3. Prosecuted O'Connell for breach of Association Act in 1831. Introduced reform bill for Ireland 1832.

Instituted Irish Board of Works. Introduced Irish Education scheme 1831. Made tithe composition compulsory 1833. Resigned as Colonial Secretary over appropriation of Church revenues. His independent party named 'Derby Dilly' by O'Connell. Compelled Whig government to modify disendowment proposals. Opposed to Peel's free-trade policy. Declined to form anti-free-trade ministry in 1846. Successful in foreign affairs in latter part of his career and Prime Minister in three administrations.

STEPHENS, JAMES (1825–1901) Civil engineer. Assisted Smith O'Brien at Ballingarry in 1848. Made unsuccessful attempt to kidnap Lord John Russell 1848. Escaped to Paris. Started Irish Republican Brotherhood in 1858 and stimulated its growth in America. Founded *Irish People* in 1863. Promised a rising in Ireland in September 1865 but was arrested. Escaped to Paris. Expelled from France in 1885 and returned to Ireland.

TANDY, JAMES NAPPER (1740–1803) Small tradesman. Attacked municipal corruption in Dublin. Supporter of American independence. Keen Volunteer. Supporter of French Revolution. Arrested 1792. Raised two battalions to agitate for reform. Fled to America. Led expedition to Donegal in 1798. Arrested in Hamburg but freed through representations of Napoleon. Died in France.

TONE, THEOBALD WOLFE (1763–98) Entered Trinity College, Dublin 1781. Called to the Irish Bar 1789. Published *Review of the Conduct of Administration* in 1790, also *Hibernicus*. Became an ardent republican. Published *An Argument on behalf of the Catholics of Ireland* 1791. Founded with Russell and Tandy the United Irishmen. Forced to go to America after conspiring with French spy. Went to Paris to prepare expedition to Ireland. Captured in 1798, court-martialled and sentenced to death. Committed suicide.

TROY, JOHN THOMAS (1739–1823) Joined Dominican Order in Rome 1756. Rector of St Clements. Bishop of Ossory 1776. Archbishop of Dublin 1784. Condemned Whiteboys. Instrumental in founding Maynooth College.

WHATELEY, RICHARD (1787–1863) M.A. Oxford 1812. D.D. 1825. Author of numerous theological tracts. Archbishop of Dublin 1831–63. Presided over commissions to administer undenominational education 1831–53. Founded Chair of Political Economy in Trinity College, Dublin 1832. Presided over commission on Irish poor 1833–6. Voted for repeal of religious tests 1835–53. Opposed to Tithe Commutation Act. Supported Maynooth Grant 1845. Did much to ease Famine distress.

SOURCES
Concise Dictionary of National Biography (DNB).
Dictionary of Modern History, ed. A. P. Walters.

CHRONOLOGY

1775 August 6. Birth of Daniel O'Connell.
Outbreak of the American Revolution.

1778 Catholic Relief Act.

1782 Legislative independence for the Irish parliament.

1788 Regency crisis.

1789 Outbreak of the French Revolution.

1790 O'Connell attends Harrington's school in Cork.

1791 O'Connell attends English College at St Omer.

1792 O'Connell attends English College at Douai.

1793 Execution of Louis XVI.
O'Connell goes to London.

1794 O'Connell enters Lincoln's Inn.

1796 O'Connell returns to Ireland.

1798 Irish rebellion.
O'Connell called to the Irish Bar.

1800 O'Connell opposes the Act of Union.

1802 O'Connell secretly marries his cousin Mary in June.

1803 Rebellion of Robert Emmet.
O'Connell's son Maurice is born.

1804 Son Morgan is born.

1805 Daughter Ellen is born.

1808 Daughter Catherine is born.

1810 Daughter Elizabeth is born, son John is born.

1813 Grattan's Catholic Relief Bill is defeated.
Trial of John Magee.

1814 Vatican announces itself favourable to veto.

1815 O'Connell kills D'Esterre in a duel.
Battle of Waterloo.

1816 Son Daniel born.

1819 O'Connell declares his support for reform if emancipation is refused.

1820 Death of George III.
Death of Henry Grattan.

1821 George IV visits Ireland.

1823 O'Connell organizes the Catholic Association.

1824 O'Connell establishes the Catholic Rent.

1825 The House of Lords vetoes Catholic relief.

1826 Waterford by-election won by Villiers Stuart.

1827 George Canning becomes Prime Minister.

1828 Peel-Wellington Ministry. O'Connell elected for Co. Clare.

1829 Catholic Emancipation Act.

1830 Death of George IV who is succeeded by William IV. O'Connell forms the Anti-Union Association. Earl Grey becomes Prime Minister.

1831 O'Connell speaks against tithes.

1834 Melbourne becomes Prime Minister. King dismisses the Whigs. Peel becomes Prime Minister.

1835 Lichfield House Compact defeats Peel. Melbourne returns as Prime Minister.

1836 Death of Mary O'Connell on October 31.

1837 Victoria succeeds William IV.

1838 O'Connell founds Precursor Society.

1839 Vatican advises bishops to avoid politics.

1840 Loyal National Repeal Association founded.

1841 O'Connell speaks to Catholics in Belfast. Becomes Lord Mayor of Dublin. Charles Gavan Duffy founds *The Nation* newspaper. Peel returns as Prime Minister.

1843 O'Connell's Monster Repeal Meetings for 'Repeal Year'. Arrested for conspiracy and convicted.

1844 O'Connell freed from Richmond Jail by House of Lords.

1845 Peel's Bill to endow Catholic charities. Potato blight strikes in the autumn.

1846 Peel replaced as Prime Minister by Lord John Russell.

1847 February 8: O'Connell's last speech in Parliament. March 22: He leaves England. May 15: Death of O'Connell at Genoa.

1848 Abortive Young Ireland rebellion.

SELECT BIBLIOGRAPHY

I ARCHIVAL SOURCES

The principal archival sources include the O'Connell papers in the National Library of Ireland and in University College, Dublin. Much personal material of Daniel O'Connell is in the possession of Lt. Col. M. O'Connell Fitz-Simon, and other sources can be secured from the relevant entries in R. Hayes's *Manuscript sources for the history of Irish civilisation* (1965).

II PRINTED CORRESPONDENCE, JOURNAL, MEMOIR AND SPEECHES

M. F. Cusack, *Speeches and public letters of the Liberator* (2 vols. 1875).

Correspondence of Daniel O'Connell, ed. W. J. Fitzpatrick (1888).

A. Houston, *Daniel O'Connell: his early life and journal, 1795–1802* (1906).

D. O'Connell, *Letters to the reformers of England on the reform bill for Ireland* (1832).

[D. O'Connell], *Memoir of the Union ... its indissolubility demonstrated* (1843).

D. O'Connell, *Memoir on Ireland, native and Saxon, 1172–1660* (3rd ed. 1885).

J. O'Connell, *The life and speeches of Daniel O'Connell MP edited by his son* (1846).

J. O'Connell, *The select speeches of Daniel O'Connell with historical notes by his son* (1856).

The correspondence of Daniel O'Connell, ed. M. O'Connell (2 vols. 1972; vol. 3, 1974). [The projected remaining volumes with those already published comprise some 3,500 letters but do not include his public letters which are included above.]

III BIOGRAPHIES

M. F. Cusack, *The Liberator: his life and times* (1872).

W. J. O'Neill Daunt, *Personal recollections of the late Daniel O'Connell, MP* (1848).

R. Dunlop, *Daniel O'Connell and the revival of national life in Ireland* (1900).

W. Fagan, *The life and times of Daniel O'Connell* (2 vols., 1847–8).

D. Gwynn, *Daniel O'Connell: the Irish liberator* (1930).

J. J. Horgan, *Great Catholic laymen: Daniel O'Connell* (1907).

W. E. H. Lecky, *The Leaders of Public Opinion in Ireland* (1903).

T. C. Luby, *Life and achievements of O'Connell* (1874).

M. Mac Donagh (the Younger), *Life of Daniel O'Connell* (1903).

M. Mac Donagh (the Younger), *Daniel O'Connell and the story of Emancipation* (1929).

A. Ó Duibhir, *Dómhnall Ó Conaill* (1949).

S. Ó Faoláin, *King of the Beggars: a life of Daniel O'Connell* (1945).

J. J. O'Kelly, *O'Connell calling: the Liberator's place in the world* (1947).

J. O'Rourke, *The centenary life of O'Connell* (1875).

D. Ó Súilleabháin, *Beatha Dhómhnaill Uí Chonaill* (1936).

M. Tierney, *Daniel O'Connell: nine centenary essays* (1949).

IV OTHER SECONDARY WORKS

J.C. Beckett, *The making of modern Ireland, 1603–1923* (1966).

J.F. Broderick, *The Holy See and repeal* (1951).

R.D. Edwards, *A new history of Ireland* (1972).

J. de La Faye, *L'Irlande au xixᵉ siècle: O'Connell, ses alliés et ses adversaires* [1896].

G.J.S. Lefevre, *Peel and O'Connell* (1887).

W.T. Mac Cullagh, *Pro-consul and tribune: Wellesley and O'Connell* (1880).

R.B. McDowell, *Public opinion and government policy, 1801–46* (1952).

A. Macintyre, *The Liberator: Daniel O'Connell and the Irish Party, 1830–47* (1965).

H.F. Mulvey, 'Nineteenth-century Ireland, 1801–1914' (*Irish Historiography 1936–70*, 1971). [Contains critical bibliography.]

K.B. Nowlan, *The politics of repeal, 1841–50* (1965).

J.A. Reynolds, *The Catholic emancipation crisis, 1823–9* (1954).

LIST AND SOURCES

Credit line in italics indicates that the photograph was provided by the institution possessing the object concerned.

Frontispiece: Portrait of Daniel O'Connell by G. J. Mulvany. Oil on canvas. Courtesy of the *National Gallery of Ireland.*

7 Inscription from the Charles Stewart Parnell monument, Dublin. Photo Bord Fáilte.

8 Portrait of Christ from the Book of Kells, fol. 32v. Early ninth century. *Trinity College, Dublin.*

10 Portrait of Henry Grattan (1746–1820). Panel by F. Wheatley, 1782. *National Portrait Gallery, London.*

11 'An Exact Representation of the Burning, Plundering and Destruction of Newgate by the Rioters, 7th June, 1780.' Engraving by H. Roberts, published 1781. Courtesy of the Trustees of the *British Museum.*

12 'The unanimous Declaration of the thirteen united States of America. In Congress, 4 July 1776. Photo United States Information Service.

14 Marble bust of George III by Edward Smyth. Courtesy of the *National Gallery of Ireland.*

15 The Viceregal Lodge, Phoenix Park, near Dublin. Engraving by

J. McGahey from *Dublin Delineated in 28 Views of the Principal Public Buildings,* 1843. *National Library of Ireland.*

16 Derrynane Abbey, Derrynane, Co. Kerry. Photo Commissioners of Public Works in Ireland.

18 Portrait of Daniel, Count O'Connell, uncle of the Liberator. Oil painting (detail). Derrynane Abbey, Co. Kerry. Photo Commissioners of Public Works in Ireland.

19 Portrait of Daniel O'Connell (1775–1847). Lithograph by Wild, published *c.* 1800. Photo Radio Times Hulton Picture Library.

21 Entry of George IV into Dublin. Aquatint by Havell. Courtesy of the *National Gallery of Ireland.*

Glass goblet commemorating the royal visit of George IV to Dublin, 1821. *National Museum of Ireland.*

22 Portrait of Arthur Wellesley, 1st Duke of Wellington. Oil on canvas by John Lucas. Courtesy of the *National Gallery of Ireland.*

23 Letter from Mary O'Connell to Daniel, 10 April 1808. Archives Department, *University College, Dublin.*

Mary O'Connell, wife of the Liberator. Oil painting (detail). Derrynane Abbey, Co. Kerry. Photo Commissioners of Public Works in Ireland.

24 Portrait of William Lamb, 2nd Viscount Melbourne. Oil on panel by G. H. Harlow. Courtesy of the *National Gallery of Ireland.*

25 Portrait of William Pitt. Mezzotint by John Jones. Courtesy of the *National Gallery of Ireland.*

26 Portrait of Charles James Fox (1749–1806). Canvas by K. A. Hickel. *National Portrait Gallery, London.*

27 The storming of the Bastille. Engraving by J. Prieur. Louvre. Photo Giraudon.

28 Bust of Theobald Wolfe Tone, founder of the United Irishmen. Photo Department of External Affairs, Dublin.

Bantry Bay. Engraving from Leitch Ritchie, *Ireland, Picturesque and Romantic,* Vol. ii, 1838. *National Library of Ireland.*

29 Engraving of the murder of Lord Kilwarden during the Emmet insurrection. Photo Radio Times Hulton Picture Library.

Portrait of Robert Emmet (1770–1832). Oil painting by John Comerford. Courtesy of the *National Gallery of Ireland.*

31 Connemara cabin, from the *Illustrated London News*, 12 August 1843. Photo *Illustrated London News.*

32 Portrait of Napoleon I in Imperial costume. Oil painting by Ingres, 1806. Musée de l'Armée, Paris. Photo Giraudon.

33 'The Union Club'. Engraving by J. Gillray, published 1801. Photo Mansell Collection.

35 The Bank of Ireland. Engraving from *Dublin Delineated in 28 Views of the Principal Public Buildings,* 1843. *National Library of Ireland.*

36 The Stuart monument. Basilica of St Peter, Rome. Photo Mansell Collection.

37 The Custom House, Dublin. Engraving by W. Woolnoth from *Dublin Delineated in 28 Views of the Principal Public Buildings,* 1843. *National Library of Ireland.*

38 Daniel O'Connell's pistols. *National Museum of Ireland.*

39 Shooting of D'Esterre. Engraving from the *Irish Magazine*, Vol. 8, 1815.

41 Statue of Edmund Burke in front of Trinity College, Dublin. Photo Green Studio Ltd, Dublin.

42 'The Repeal Farce, or Mother Goose and the Golden Eggs.' Cartoon from *Punch*, Vol. IV, 1843, p. 37. Reproduced by permission of *Punch.*

43 Silver button by Hardiman and Iliffes agitating for Repeal, 1844. *National Museum of Ireland.*

44 Medal by Isaac Parkes (obverse and reverse) commemorating Daniel O'Connell's election as MP for Clare, 1828. *National Museum of Ireland*

45 Statue of James Warren Doyle, Bishop of Kildare and Leighlin. Courtesy of the Reverend Administrator, Carlow Cathedral.

46 Portrait of Charles, 2nd Earl Grey. Canvas after T. Lawrence, *c.* 1828. *National Portrait Gallery, London.*

49 'The Irish ogre fattening on the "Finest Pisantry".' Cartoon from *Punch*, Vol. VI, 1844, p. 15. Reproduced by permission of *Punch.*

White metal unsigned medal commemorating Daniel O'Connell and the Reform Bill, 1832. *National Museum of Ireland.*

50 'King O'Connell at Tara.' Cartoon from *Punch*, Vol. VI, 1844, p. 89. Reproduced by permission of *Punch.*

51 Letter from Daniel O'Connell to his wife (detail), 20 October 1802. *National Library of Ireland.*

52 Mr O'Connell's residence, Merrion Square, Dublin. Engraving from the *Illustrated London News*, 18 November 1843. Photo *Illustrated London News.*

54 'The Irish Frankenstein.' Cartoon from *Punch*, Vol. VI, 1844, p. 199. Reproduced by permission of *Punch.*

55 Portrait of Edward Stanley. Watercolour on ivory by an unknown artist. Courtesy of the *National Gallery of Ireland.*

56 Portrait of Sir Robert Peel, Bt (1788–1850). Panel by J. Linnell, 1838. *National Portrait Gallery, London.*

57 Portrait of Thomas Drummond. Oil on canvas by H. W. Pickersgill. Courtesy of the *National Gallery of Ireland.*

59 'A Daniel – a Daniel Come to Judgement!' Cartoon from *Punch*, 1842. Photo Mansell Collection.

'The Modern Sisyphus.' Cartoon from *Punch*, 1843. Reproduced by permission of *Punch.*

60 'Brother, brother, we're both in the wrong.' Cartoon from *Punch*, Vol. V, 1843, p. 255. Reproduced by permission of *Punch.*

61 Portrait of Archbishop John MacHale, 1855. Oil on canvas by Alessandro Capalti. Courtesy of the *National Gallery of Ireland.*

62 Portrait of Charles Gavan Duffy. Oil on canvas by Franklin after O'Neill. Courtesy of the *National Gallery of Ireland.*

63 Weekly meeting of the Repeal Association, Corn Exchange, Dublin. Engraving from the *Illustrated London News*, 19 August 1843. Photo *Illustrated London News.*

Repeal meeting at Tara. Engraving from the *Illustrated London News*, 26 August 1843. Photo *Illustrated London News.*

64 Mr O'Connell, in his triumphal car. Engraving from the *Illustrated*

INDEX

(1800) 30–1, 34, 43, 83; and American War of Independence 11–13; and annual tribute 57–8; biographical attitudes to 91, 94; birth of 11–12, 16; centenary celebrations of 90; and Catholic Church and clergy 20–2, 31, 43, 46, 62, 68, 78, 88–90; and Catholic emancipation 19–22, 34, 38–9, 43–4, 48–9, 52, 55, 69, 83, 88; and Catholicism 30; and Catholics 35, 44–5, 49, 52, 60, 70; character of 18–22, 39, 44–5, 66, 68–9, 76; childhood of 18; children of 23, 24–5, 68, 70; Clare election (1828) 44–5, 49; Clontarf monster meeting and 64, 78, 81, 92; correspondence of 23; death of 69, 81, 89; Derrynane Abbey and 22; D'Esterre, John Norcot and 38–9; Dublin Castle and 70; and education in Ireland 55, 80, 89; education of 17, 19; and elections 44–5, 48–9, 61; and emigration 70, 72, 75; and Emmet, Robert 29, 31; and English Catholics 22, 48, 51; and English public opinion 22, 70, 72, 77; and English society 51–2; and evictions 74–5; European recognition of 49–50, 88; and family 17, 23; and famine in Ireland 68, 70, 72, 75–6, 81; and feminine society 19, 23–5; finances of 22–4, 57–8; and forty-shilling freeholders 22, 49, 74; and French revolution 29–30; and George IV 21–2; and Gaelic tradition 18, 86, 88; imprisonment of 64, 66, 80; and Ireland, administration of 70, 75; and Irish Catholic Association 21, 47–8; and Irish Catholic Committee 30, 43; and Irish self-government 29–30, 34–5, 44; and Kerry 24, 61, 68; as a 'king' 50; and landlords 48, 75; as a landlord 76; as a law student 17–18, 31; as a lawyer 19–20, 29, 38–9, 48–9, 57, 78; as a leader 20, 38, 47, 81, 86; 'Liberator' 22; and Lichfield House Compact 55–6, 62; and John Mac-Hale, Archbishop of Tuam 62; marriage with Mary O'Connell 22–4, 52, 60–1; and meetings (public and monster) 20, 39, 45, 61, 64, 78; monarchy, attitude of 18; Moore's *Irish Melodies* 86–7; and *The Nation* 62, 66, 68, 80; and nationalism 35, 44, 62, 66, 72, 76, 81, 83, 88, 91, 94; and 'no popery' 22; obsequies of 89; and O'Connell, Maurice 'Hunting Cap' 17, 19; and Orange Order 47, 55, 77; papers of 18–19; and Parliament 44, 52, 74; and

Peel, Sir Robert 47, 67, 78; and Penal Laws 30; and politics 29, 58; and Poor Law 70, 75; and Precursor Society 60; and Protestants 30, 43, 47, 51–2, 70, 77, 81, 83, 91–2, 94; and Reform bill 70; and religion 21, 31, 58, 61, 76; and repeal 34, 42, 45–7, 50–2, 55, 58, 61–2, 64, 66, 68–70, 76–8, 80–1, 83, 87–8, 92, 95; and Repeal Year 64; and republicanism 16, 30, 44; and revolution 30, 34, 42, 45, 72, 76, 78, 80; and Scotland 48; and society 19; and tenants 76; and tithes 45, 52, 70; and trade unions 78, 80; and Ulster 52, 69, 77, 91–2; and United Irishmen 29, 31; and 'Whig interpretation of history' 43–4; and Whig policy 22, 44, 55, 58, 68, 70, 74, 76, 81; and Young Irelanders 62, 66, 68, 80–1, 88–9

*O'Connell, Daniel Charles, Count 16–19
O'Connell, Daniel Robert 16
O'Connell, family of 16–18, 33
O'Connell, 'Hunting Cap' *see* O'Connell, Maurice
*O'Connell, Mary 22–4, 51, 60
*O'Connell, Maurice 'Hunting Cap' 16–19, 22, 29–31
O'Connell, Maurice R., Professor 22, 24, 57
O'Connell, Morgan (father) 16
O'Connellism 90–2
*O'Conor, Charles, of Bellanagare 85
O'Donovan, John 17
*O'Halloran, Sylvester 85
O'Neill, Hugh 44
O'Neill, Shane 44
Orangemen 55, 77, 92
Orange Order 47, 57, 77, 92
Ossian, by Macpherson 18, 84–7
Ossianic movement 84, 87

Paine, Thomas 13
Paisley, Rev. Ian 94
papacy 9, 16–17, 36, 44, 47, 90
Parliament, at Westminster 31, 44, 60
parliamentary organization 17, 40–1, 48
parliamentary reform 27–8, 41, 43–4, 48–9, 51, 54
*Parnell, Charles Stewart 90, 93, 95
*Parnell, Henry, 20
Peel, Sir Robert 44, 55–6, 61–2, 72, 76, 81; and administration of Ireland 58, 66–8, 76; and Catholic emancipation 46; and O'Connell 51, 64, 70; and repeal 78, 80
Penal Laws 15, 17, 30

Pitt, William, the younger 25–6, 36
Plantagenets 9
Poor Law 58, 70, 75
*Portland, William Henry Cavendish Bentinck, third Duke of 26
Precursor Society 60
Presbyterians 35, 55, 82–3
Prince Regent 26, 36; *see also* George IV
Protestant ascendancy 30, 40–1, 70, 81
Protestantism 21, 52, 55, 57
Protestants 8–9, 47, 77, 82–3, 92, 94

Queens Colleges 80, 88–9

rebellion 73, 78, 88
Redmond, John E. 93
Reform Bill (1832) 49, 54–5, 70, 76
reform bills 58
Regency crisis 26
regium donum 35
repeal 34, 45–7, 49, 51, 55, 61, 68, 76, 87, 89, 95; movements 58, 62, 83, 88, 92
repealers 64, 88
republicanism 15, 26, 30, 42, 44, 89
Republic of Ireland 93
revolution 47, 93; of 1688–9 10, 26, 40; in America 12, 85
Richmond Jail, Dublin 64
Rinuccini, John Baptist 16
Rising (1916) 91, 94
Romans 33
Rome 9; and Irish politics 20, 37, 43, 52, 91; and O'Connell 50, 69, 81, 89; *see also* Catholic Church, papacy
Russell, Lord John 56, 68, 89–90

St Omer 17
St Patrick 30
Salamanca 36
Scotland 9, 36, 92
Scott, Sir Walter 21
Seven Years War 12
*Sheehan, Remigius 50–1
*Sheehy, Father Nicholas 41
smuggling 17
social contract 81
South America, wars of independence in 68
Spain 38
*Stanley, Edward, fourteenth Earl of Derby 55
Stephens, James 90
Stuart, House of 9, 17–18, 36, 85; and Catholics 10, 15, 40
Stuart, John, third Earl of Bute 85